From Rage
to Responsibility

Black Conservative
Jesse Lee Peterson
and America Today

Jesse Lee Peterson
with Brad Stetson

Foreword by Dennis Prager

PARAGON HOUSE
St. Paul, Minnesota

First Edition, 2000

Published in the United States by
Paragon House
2700 University Avenue West
St. Paul, MN 55114

Acknowledgement is given to Prager Publishers, an imprint of the Greenwood Publishing Group, Inc. for permission to print passages from the following works by Brad Stetson, *The Silent Subject: Reflections on the Unborn in American Culture* (1996), *Black and Right: The Bold New Face of Black Conservatives in America* (1997), and *Human Dignity and Contemporary Liberalism* (1998).

Manufactured in the United States of America.

Library of Congress Cataloging-in-Publication Data

Peterson, Jesse Lee, 1949-
     From rage to responsibility: Black conservative Jesse Lee Peterson and America today
     / by Jesse Lee Peterson with Brad Stetson; foreword by Dennis Prager.-- 1 st ed.
          p. cm.
     Includes bibliographical references (p.) and index.
     ISBN 1-55778-788-3 (cloth)
       1. United States--Race relations. 2. United States--Social conditions--1980- 3. Peterson,
     Jesse Lee, 1949---Political and social views. 4. Social problems--United States.
     5. Social values--United States. 6. Conservatism--United States. 7. Peterson, Jesse
     Lee, 1949- 1. Stetson, Brad. II. Title.

E185.615 .P437 2000
305.8'00973--dc21

                                                                              00-020813

For current information about all releases from Paragon House,
visit the web site at http://www.paragonhouse.com

To the young people of B.O.N.D. for their willingness and courage to take on the challenges of life, and thereby setting an example for others to see.

To the men and women of B.O.N.D. who have dedicated themselves to change, and who have selflessly volunteered their time, financial resources, and prayer to bring this message of truth to not only black Americans, but all Americans.

To the staff of B.O.N.D. for their total commitment to this cause. None of our accomplishments, including this book, would be possible without their extraordinary efforts.

I think on a larger level the idea of a black conservative is disturbing to liberals. It does not confirm their sense of their own virtue. Their virtue is, in many ways, tied to this idea that blacks are victims who have to be helped. And the black conservative is someone who, in a sense, says "No," we have to really be responsible for ourselves, whether or not you help. So, the black conservative makes the liberal feel obsolete, irrelevant on some level. Aside from the obvious ideological disagreements the two might have, there's this, I think, in the liberal sense, that, "If I really go along with you and accept that, then my own politics, my own idea of virtuousness becomes obsolete."

—*Shelby Steele*

Jesse Lee Peterson

JESSE LEE PETERSON is a radio/television talk show host, successful entrepreneur, author, speaker, and the Founder/President of the national non-profit organization, Brotherhood Organization of A New Destiny (B.O.N.D.), whose purpose is "Rebuilding the Family by Rebuilding the Man." Mr. Peterson is a board member of the National Grassroots Alliance and is on the advisory board of Project 21. He lives in California.

CONTENTS

FOREWORD

In a society that regularly confuses fame with significance, Jesse Peterson's significance may not be readily apparent because he does not yet have the fame that he deserves. But this man has touched more souls more deeply than almost any famous person in America today.

That is why I felt so honored when he asked if I would write the foreword to his book, *From Rage to Responsibility*.

In his daily life, his daily work, and in this book, Jesse Peterson exemplifies two qualities rare in any age, and certainly rare in our own: a passion for truth and extraordinary courage. There are many pages in this book that cry out to be proclaimed to America. As I read the book, particularly those chapters dealing with race, victimhood, and rage, I kept thinking, "I must read this aloud on my radio show."

If the media anointed Jesse Peterson America's spokesman on race, replacing those they have thus far anointed, whatever racial tensions America suffers would decrease to the point of virtual nonexistence. For the racial truth of America is beautiful and ugly at the same time. The beautiful truth is that despite pockets of racism, America is essentially the least racist multiethnic society in the world. The ugly truth is that acknowledgement of this would devastate the civil rights movement and decimate the Democratic Party.

Encouraging and defending black rage is the *sine qua non* of the civil rights movement and the Democratic Party. A black without rage, a happy black American, is less likely to be a liberal black American. If too many black Americans come to be at peace with their society one of our two great parties would have little chance of attaining national power. With regard to race, Orwellian doublespeak, e.g., "race consciousness is moral, race blindness is racist," is our dominant language. And Jesse Peterson is one of our Orwells.

Whatever the issue, Jesse seeks truth and speaks with courage. Even on the few matters that I may not entirely agree with Jesse, he forces me to think a second and a third time. He is so morally grounded and fearless that when we differ, my first reaction is to ask myself, "Where did I go wrong?"

I have but one regret: that every reader cannot know Jesse Peterson personally. It is just plain sad that he cannot visit the home of each of his readers. The reader would meet one of the handful of great men anyone is privileged to meet in a lifetime. Those of us who know him are better able to appreciate the biblical view of man as "created in the image of God." Indeed that is his entire message in a nutshell, that only when we recognize that all people are made in God's image will we move from rage to responsibility—the responsibility of acting as the God of the Ten Commandments wants us to act.

—Dennis Prager

PREFACE

It is not a sign of weakness, but a sign of high maturity to rise to a level of self-criticism.

—Martin Luther King, Jr.

Can you remember how you felt in school, after you figured out a math problem, or some other question that had been vexing you? Do you remember how excited you were to finally "get it," and how badly you wanted to share the answer with your friends, and explain to them how you solved the problem?

Well, that's how I feel about the issues I discuss in this book. Whether it is black Americans' attitudes about racism, the difficulties men and women have getting along with each other, abortion, education, immigration or the path back to national greatness, I eagerly want to share with you what I think are helpful and valuable insights.

That is why, after spending ten years doing counseling and grassroots community work with my non-profit black empowerment organization B.O.N.D. (Brotherhood Organization of a New Destiny)—as well as debating on talkradio and traveling the national lecture circuit—I've produced this book. I want to tell you about the personally healing and politically important truths I've discovered, in the belief that they will be of practical assistance to you in your life.

But of course whenever anyone tells their own story, there is the danger of dwelling too heavily on minor personal details, of preening like a rock star, and thereby losing sight of what is truly significant and helpful about one's history.

In order to avoid this mistake, in this book I say comparatively little about myself, and instead concentrate on the ideas and values that have shaped me, and which, I hope, will be of assistance to others. After chapter one, which gives the salient details of my childhood and the major events in my life, I focus on the principles and values that define my politics, occasionally integrating into their exposition elements of my own individual experience as a critic of liberalism and the race-conscious politics it has given us. This makes for a book that combines the private and the public in a narrative weave, illustrating how one's life experiences—in childhood and adulthood—can influence one's political orientation and participation, for good or ill.

In these pages you will find a "black conservative in action," frankly examining ideas, fighting stereotypes, attacking the numbing complacency so prevalent in our country when it comes to thinking about race and social issues. It is my hope that my journey from rage to responsibility will be as personally and politically liberating for you as it has proven to be for me.

I wish you peace.

Chapter One

MY STORY

You are a traitor to your race! What is the matter with you, thinking like a white man! You are a boot-lickin' Uncle Tom, and you hate black people. How can you give aid and comfort to the enemy of your own people by talking like a conservative? I pity your mama, boy. Where do you come from anyway?
—*A black man in the audience heckling Jesse Lee Peterson during one of his speeches.*

Judging by how angry that man was at me, you would think I came straight from the pit of Hell. He certainly thought so. Now, I used to badmouth sleepy little Comer Hill, Alabama, as a lot of things, but Hell wasn't one of them. Although, like Hell, I suppose, it was hot, dry and dull.

It was the Spring of 1949, in the days of Jim Crow, when my mama gave birth to me on a former plantation in Comer Hill, between Montgomery and Tuskeegee. My family had worked that land for years. In fact, my great-grandparents and their parents had worked there as slaves. In a lot of ways, that farm was all my family had ever known. I can still remember as a very young child, having to go with my grandmother and siblings up to the big white house on the hill, and clean it up in preparation for the return of the plantation owners. They were people I never really knew, and they didn't have much to do with us. But I do remember this: neither my grandmother, with whom I lived, nor my grandfather, who managed the farm and lived down the road, ever complained about the owner. They never spoke behind their backs. This, even though there was a history in Comer Hill of white people attacking us.

The most notorious case of racist violence against us involved my grandmother's father. He was a tall, burly fellow who was known throughout Comer Hill as being outspoken and blunt, even to whitefolk. He was the manager of the plantation in his day, and apparently angered the white owners of the other plantations in the area by hiring a renegade black worker.

This black man, who worked on one farm, came to my great-grandfather looking for work on the farm he ran, and my great-granddad hired him. I guess this was a breach of some kind of plantation etiquette, because a group of white owners came after my great-granddad. Fortunately, he was known by everyone in Comer Hill to be good with a gun; this kept the white men away from him for awhile.

But one night, they came to his house and surprised him, and when he went for his gun, which he kept under his bed, it wasn't there. His wife had, for some reason, moved it to a different place in the house, without telling him. So they busted into the house and yanked him outside. They shot him straight away, before he could even defend himself. They were yelling "Nigger" the whole time, cursing him for hiring a man looking for work. No one was ever arrested for this murder. No one was ever held accountable in any way.

Growing Up

But by the time I came along in Comer Hill, things had calmed down a bit. Of course the attitudes were still racist, it was Jim Crow after all. And anytime we went into a town, there were the segregated water fountains, bathrooms, parks, and such. That's the way life was, and that's the way people lived then. It was wrong, and we knew it. Still, though, we found ways to get by, and there was one resource we relied on more than anything else: family.

Like many black families from the poor South, mine is extended and complicated. In my early years, it was my grandfather who was the central figure in my life. He was a brown skinned man, tall and lean, with the broad shoulders and leathery, callused hands that came from a lifetime of picking cotton and doing plantation work. I still remember the fearful respect his deep, powerful voice would stir in me whenever he would call me. "Punchie, come here now," he would say, in a booming voice that sounded to my young ears like thunder. Everyone called me Punchie. I don't really know why, my grandmother said it was because I was an active baby, rolling and bopping, always moving. But when my grandfather called you, you came, no matter if he used your name or not.

Looking back on it now, this man must have been an expert on child-rearing, because all together, he had at least 13 kids, and nobody, I mean nobody, ever got out of line with him. If you did, he was quick with the switch, and there was no talking your way out of it.

I once made the mistake of not coming quickly enough when he called me. When I finally reached him, I knew he was upset. When he became upset he would get a distant, smoldering look in his eyes, and he would slowly purse his lips, over and over. I started stammering something, but he interrupted me, and said in a matter of fact way, "You're gonna learn to come when I call, boy," and then, before I could say anything else, "Whap!," right across my behind, he hit me with the switch he had with him. So, without any benefit of a college degree, a lecture from a social worker, or any kind of advice from a trained "childcare professional," this old man controlled all of us, decently but firmly.

He was not married to my grandmother, with whom he had six kids, nor was he married to the lady down the road with whom he had five kids. He was married to his wife, though, who lived still further down the road, and he had two children by her. So altogether, his 13 kids and three women lived and worked together on this plantation. We were a very extended family but got along well, sticking close by each other and working.

Although I loved my grandfather, he was emotionally remote, mainly a disciplinary force, and I was not especially close to him. I spent most of my early years with my grandmother, who really doted on me. I was born with a cleft palate, which I didn't have repaired until I was in my late teens, so she felt, I think, a special attachment to me. She took wonderful care of me. But throughout those early years, I was haunted by the fact that I did not know who my father was, and I did not have a father in my life. I saw other kids who had close relationships with their fathers, and I missed that. There was a huge void in my life as a child, a gnawing pain that constantly distracted and preoccupied me. I felt like I couldn't explain to myself who I was.

Hunger for Father

For all of my childhood I had an unusually big head, larger than anyone else in my family, and I always wondered why. The kids at school were always ridiculing me about my noggin, and my cleft palate. I could deal with being teased about my cleft palate and the speech impediment it caused, but I was genuinely bothered about the size of my head. "How did this happen to me?", I would wonder when I was alone, placing my hands on either side of my head and pushing in, thinking I would be able to compress it to a normal size. I felt a lot of anxiety over the absence of a father in my life, and I used to yearn, to literally ache in my gut, for him to come into my life and make himself known to me, and claim me as his son. I felt his presence would give order to my life, help me understand myself, and enable me to deal with the adversity of my experience.

Then, when I was about 13, it happened. It was just a normal slow summer Saturday in Comer Hill, and I was wandering through the yard throwing stones around. There wasn't much else to do. Suddenly I heard my grandmother call "Punchie!" with an unusual sense of urgency. I hurried back to the house.

As I walked in the door, I saw her standing next to a man about 30 years old, about six feet tall, well-built and handsome. I stopped and looked at him. He stepped toward me, and leaned over a little bit and said, looking straight into my eyes, "Boy, my name is Cullen, I'm your father."

I didn't say anything, but my stomach dropped to my feet, my eyes widened and my heart skipped a beat as I stared at him and watched him talk to my grandmother. As I looked at him, I felt so many feelings at once: embarrassment, elation, satisfaction, contentment, curiosity. I was indescribably excited he had come to see me, but I did not know how to react to his attention.

I gazed at him, studying the way he looked. His appearance explained to me where I got my big head. I'd never seen another man with a head as big as his. I saw other bits of myself reflected in his body: the small ears, the wiry frame, the long face. As I studied him, I felt completed, like a missing piece of my life had been supplied to me, a stabilizing knowledge had come into me.

He gave me ten dollars when he left, and told me to come visit him where he lived, in the town of East Chicago, Indiana. I can still remember the feeling of exhilaration I felt after he left, as though I were the center of the universe. I felt somehow bigger, as though a part of my identity had been supplied to me, some self-knowledge that had previously been missing. I don't mean to say that the simple fact that he was my biological father meant more to me than the love I'd received from my grandmother and other family, not at all. It was not raw biology that moved me. Instead, it was the natural awareness I had that a father is critically important to a child, and that a boy needs his father with him, to help him grow into a man. I had a sense, even as a child, that a woman alone (mother, grandmother, auntie, whatever), was not best for a child. So it was that intuition about the importance of fathers, as well as the reality that I had always had a strong feeling of personal loss concerning my father (I didn't know who he was, if he existed, or what he thought about me), that fueled my fascination and elation with him. Having him come to me and identify himself, gave me a feeling of validation and importance, as though I meant enough to him for him to come forward and acknowledge me. Of course, the man should have done much more than that, long before then. But at age 13, meandering into manhood in Comer Hill, I was grateful for what had happened.

And indeed, during my teen years I took my father up on his

offer, and I would occasionally go up to Indiana for short visits, usually a few weeks or so, during the summers. I loved hanging around my father those few weeks a year, going around with him as he met his friends, being introduced to them as his son. It was meaningful to me. He owned a small clothes cleaning business, and once he took me to his business and introduced me to his employees. "This is my son, Punchie," he would tell them, patting me on the back. When he would do that, my whole body would tingle.

But I had to see my father behind my mother's back. She hated my father for reasons I didn't understand at the time, so she tried to keep me from him, and discouraged me from ever seeing him. I would go anyway, secretly.

My mother lived near East Chicago at that time, in the city of Gary, with her husband (my stepfather), and my eight younger siblings, all of whom were the children of my stepfather by my mother. I was the only child my mother had by my father. She had moved to Gary when I was a toddler. Around Comer Hill she met and married the man who was to be my stepfather, and she wanted to start a new life with him in Gary, so she left me in Comer Hill with her mother.

Those summers in Gary were good for me for a lot of reasons, not the least of which was I discovered why my mother and stepfather had always been so cold to me. Having met my father, I realized how much I looked like him. Of course, my mother realized it long ago, and in her mind that likeness—along with the anger she had for my father—caused her to reject me. My stepfather tried hard to be kind and loving to me, but I wanted my real father, and that overwhelming reality, along with the rest of our family circumstances, made it difficult for him and me to get along. I was not his son, I knew it, and he knew it. I didn't look like him, I hadn't lived with him very long, and, deep down I think, he associated me with a rival suitor, my father. So to both my mother and my stepfather, I represented the bad memory of my father, and it was not a pleasant association for either one of them.

There was one incident, which I did not learn of until I was an adult, that helped me understand much of my family's hostility, especially my mother's anger toward me, and why she was never able to truly love me as a child. When she became pregnant with me, she was 17, and so was my father. My mother had never been with another man, but my father, wishing to evade the responsibility of fatherhood, denied he was my father when my mother informed him she was pregnant. He told my mother, "You're pregnant by another man, you've been with someone else, because that baby is not mine."

This remark, spread around their circle of friends by my father, infuriated my mother. She had not been promiscuous, and the suggestion that she had was more than she could take. Her rage and anger at my father burned my whole childhood, and it lasts to this day. And because, as a child, I looked so much like my father, her hostility toward him was directed at me. She was, in many ways, a slave to her anger at my father, and this emotion was so dominant in her life it prevented her from fulfilling one of the most basic functions of any human being: parenting one's own children. Her anger at him kept her from loving me.

So it was especially difficult for me when, just before my last two years of high school, I moved up to Gary to live with my mother. My grandmother thought it would be better for me to go to school in urban Gary, rather than rural Alabama. The times were tough there in Gary for me, though, because I could sense she and my stepfather didn't really want me around. Often I'd visit and stay over at my father's place, where I felt more welcomed.

Further making life difficult for me in Gary, was the high school I attended, Edison High. It was incredibly violent. I had never seen anything like it. It was a frightening place, and it was there, for the first time, that I saw black people fighting other black people. They would tangle on the playground, in the hallways, in front of school after dismissal, wherever. None of the administrators at the school had the courage to try to stop it. Fighting became a sort of expected student activity. It shook me to see that, though, because in relatively innocent Comer Hill, disputes rarely got to the point of blows.

But it was a very different culture in Gary, and I was not pre-
pared for it. I managed to stay out of trouble myself, but it was a
constant effort. My country accent and cleft palate—along with
the speech impediment it caused—made me an easy target for
bullies. Confused young men showed off their "manhood" by
making fun of me in public. At one point I had to stop riding the
bus home, because of the severity with which other students
taunted me. Plus, there were fights between black students literally every day on the bus. They used to call them "bus battles." It
was a dangerous place to be, it seemed like a rolling prison.

The black students there were dedicated not to studying, but
to anger and destruction. I didn't see the point of that, so I ended
up being best friends with one of the few white students there,
because he was the only person I could find who controlled himself. This, of course, only further antagonized my black peers toward me. I was regularly chided for "trying to be white," simply
because I had made friends with a white person, and wasn't interested in fighting. After my first year in Gary, I moved back to
the Comer Hill area to finish high school, because I just couldn't
stand it at Edison High anymore.

Lost Years

After graduating from high school, I came out to California to
be with my uncle and aunt. It was the summer of 1968. I had
been out to California once before, and I loved it so much, I
wanted to come back. So my uncle, as a favor, pulled some strings
and got me a job at the Better Foods Market at Slauson and
Western, in South-Central Los Angeles. I boxed groceries and
took some classes at Los Angeles City College. But since I had
to hitchhike to the school, I began to come into contact with all
kinds of unsavory characters. Drugs were plentiful and hip at the
time, and soon I got involved. It was marijuana mostly, often
offered to me by the people who picked me up hitchhiking. I
remember thinking it was amazing the number of people who

smoked "weed" while driving a car in LA.

I was a confused young man, wandering through life. I worked at Sears, I worked as a janitor, I held all kinds of odd jobs. Eventually I moved away from my uncle and aunt, around age 23, and went on welfare. The people I hung out with on the streets told me that if you were black and went to a welfare office claiming to be a drug addict and unable to function, you would be given money. It was a scam that was guaranteed to succeed, I was assured, so I tried it.

Sure enough, it worked, and I had instant money. My take was $300 a month, plus rent money, food stamps, and vocational training. I was amazed at how easy it was. Every month, the money rolled in. The first effect of this generosity—without any kind of accountability—was that I stopped even trying to work. And of course, since I wasn't working, I started partying more. I started experimenting with drugs and sex, and descended into a pit of irresponsibility and laziness. It nearly destroyed me.

Around this same time, I regularly listened to Louis Farrakhan. He was not very well-known nationally at that time, but people in South-Central LA knew him, and he was popular. He was like your sassy cousin, who always said the stuff you wanted to say, but were too afraid. He talked about how great blacks were, how noble our ancestry was, and how white people stole mathematics and virtually all the rest of Western Civilization from us. My neighborhood friends and I would often gather around a radio, listen together, and cheer him on. And, usually, just as Farrakhan had his audience all pumped up, he would say the "blue eyed devil," the white man, is now keeping you from realizing the wealth and success that should be yours. We blacks were, to Farrakhan, victims of the conniving, scheming white man. Sitting around, on drugs and welfare, we were eager to agree with him.

Hearing Farrakhan and his powerful anger inspired me. It made me feel good to be black. It also caused me to hate the white people around me, and to be suspicious of them. He taught me they were my enemy, they could not be trusted, and I should have as little as possible to do with them. I began to truly hate and resent them. Whenever I saw a white person driving a nice car, I'd curse them, and whenever I'd pass a white person on the street, I'd give them my most menacing stare. Whenever I had a disagreement with anybody white, I automatically ascribed it to racism and bigotry on their part. Farrakhan's message had schooled me in hate. I was a seething cauldron of anger at white people. In fact, looking back on it, Farrakhan then, as now, did not mainly cause within black people a love for other black people, but rather a hatred of non-blacks.

The resentment Farrakhan peddled to me was like a drug, it seeped deep down into my system. This destructive emotion was only reinforced by the rhetoric of black politicians, whose most basic assumption, it seemed to me, was that American society was hopelessly racist. Racism was all around me, I thought, and I began to wonder what was the point of trying to work hard and do well if "Whitey" was just going to take it all away from me anyway. This was the early seventies, the heyday of the Black Panthers and various other kinds of black agitators, all selling basically the same message of anger, bitterness and revenge against the white establishment.

So, spurred by those influences, all the way up until my mid-thirties, I was a sullen, furious and racist black man. While my young childhood seemed in some ways idyllic, the realities of urban black life had turned me into a brooding and unproductive person. I lived in a culture of hostility, and the only satisfaction I could find was in the temporary highs of drugs, alcohol and sex. These things provided no real satisfaction to me at all, though. They never do, of course. I thought all of my problems were external to myself, and beyond my power to fix. I felt I had been victimized by an unfair society. I was passive, expecting the government and politicians to create ways for me to succeed. My battle was with American society, I was certain, and not with myself.

By 1988, I was approaching my fortieth year of life, and I had nothing to show for it but a lot of confusion and wasted time. I sensed an emptiness in my life, a lack of substance to myself. I sensed I was a weak man and a lost soul, with very little true understanding of myself, values, and human nature.

Recovery

I had for years been attending many different black churches throughout my neighborhood, and, although I could talk Christianity, like most of my neighbors, I had never lived it. In fact, I didn't know anybody who actually lived the Christian Gospel we all so enthusiastically shouted about on Sunday. Ironically, it was through the radio, the same medium that introduced me to the exhilarating rage of Louis Farrakhan, that I started back on the road to responsibility.

I heard a minister and popular psychologist named Roy Masters talking about human hatred and the destructiveness it brings to peoples' lives. He recommended praying to God, quietly and simply, and asking for understanding about one's life. So I tried it. I didn't ask God for anything material, I just sought to know myself, and to better comprehend the path I was on. It was a simple prayer, but one I prayed fervently.

After a few weeks, I began to feel much differently about myself. I felt a new understanding taking hold of me, a kind of self-knowledge I had not known before. I realized the depth of my anger and resentment, and the havoc and discontent it had sewn in my life. I also, for the first time, saw clearly who my anger was ultimately directed towards: my parents.

I was angry at my father for abandoning me, and not showing me by intimate example what it meant to be a man; I was angry at my mother for hating me, and not giving me the tender love and nurturing a child needs; I was angry at my stepfather for rejecting me; I was angry at white people for their racism, and I was angry at American society for everything else. Deep down, I was also angry at God for the way my life was. I was angry at everybody and everything, except myself.

When I understood that, and saw how ridiculous it was, I began to feel differently. The dark void in my heart began to glimmer with the light of hope, and the emptiness inside of me was replaced with the beginnings of self-knowledge. I saw that the basic source of my discontent was my mind, the attitudes I had chosen, and not what other people had done to me. I saw that I was free to decide for myself the kind of person I was going to be, and that I did not have to accept the script of rage written for me by the "black leaders" of the day. I saw they were leading me nowhere but into dependence on them and the state, and offering me nothing in return but some angry sound-bites by which to organize my life. I realized that I could think for myself, and that "The Black Experience" was a myth used to control black people. I resolved then to be mentally independent, to think for myself and live as an individual, not as a part of some racial clan.

As I prayed and came to understand myself, seeing the habits of thinking I had developed, I began to feel genuinely sorry for hating my parents. I knew it was wrong. True, they had not given me the love and support they should have, but I was an adult now, and the course my life had taken was my doing, not theirs. I was responsible for what I had become, not my parents, who, after all, were just flawed human beings like everyone else. I felt a tremendous burden to make things right with them, and to establish a normal, friendly relationship. Not that we would pretend we all were great pals, or forget that the past had been hurtful, but simply to establish that there was no bitter grudge on my part toward them.

Reconciliation

As it happened, around this time—about Spring 1988—my mother was in California, visiting my aunt on a vacation. So I resolved to meet with her. I felt compelled to do it. I can still clearly remember today the intense fear I felt as I approached my auntie's house. My heart was pounding, and my palms were sweating as I walked toward her door. I knew it was the right thing to do, but still, anxiety gripped me. I hadn't seen my mother in several years, and I didn't know how she would react. After I walked in and greeted my mother and aunt, I asked my mother if I could talk to her privately. She looked apprehensive, but she agreed.

We both went into a bedroom, and sat on the edge of a bed. I faced her and said to her firmly, "Mama, I want to tell you I'm sorry for hating you, and being angry at you my whole life. I should not have done that. I want you to know I love you, and hold nothing against you." As soon as I said it, I felt tremendously liberated. I saw her cry for the first time ever. She told me she was sorry she had not been a better mother to me, and that she should not have allowed her anger at my father to be transferred to me. It was a beautiful and emancipating discussion, and when I left, I knew that I had done something morally good. I felt that I had faced my fear and resentment, and broken its control over my life. I knew I had expressed a personal maturity I had lacked for most of my life, and it was very gratifying.

Later, in the summer of 1988, I went back to East Chicago to make things right with my father. I wish I had been able to do the same with my stepfather, but he had died several years earlier, while I was wasting my life in L. A. To this day, my heart aches that I was not able to see him, and talk with him one last time.

But fortunately, I did make it to my father in time. When I saw him, I told him that I had forgiven him, and was not going to hold anything against him. He was open to me, and grateful for the heart to heart talk, and the healing it brought. When I left Gary that summer I understood that by God's grace I had become a solid man even without the tutelage of my father or stepfather, and that, in a strange way, maybe I learned more about the importance of fathers by not having one.

That year was a healing time for me. I knew the forgiveness I had shown was right, pleasing to God, and the mark of a true Christian. Without even realizing it, I had begun to live the Christianity I had spent much of my life merely talking and singing about. I felt like I had rooted hypocrisy out of my life, and come to inward peace. "The Gospel is something to be lived, not just talked about," I had once heard a preacher say, and now I had the satisfaction of knowing that I had developed some important habits of obedience.

In late 1989 I started my own janitorial service, and that gave me a lot of time to think. Empty workshops, offices and meeting rooms were my own private forum, as late at night I would think out loud, and speak my mind to the quiet desks and chairs. I reflected on my life, and the lives of the people I knew, and I came to see some clear patterns at work. I saw that my troubles— like so many of my black friends'—centered on fatherlessness. I had not been provided with a model of masculinity and the life-lessons that a father can give a son, and this was the basic source of my anger. I also resented my mother's anger at me, an anger brought on by her resentment of being abandoned by my father.

So it was my anger at my father for leaving me, my mother's anger at him for leaving her—an anger she also channeled at me and which I returned to her—that all converged and set the stage in my life for an enduring hostility. This vicious cycle of personal resentment was only made worse by the tutoring in political anger provided to me by the black community in Gary and later in Los Angeles. Basically my whole adulthood was spent in a culture of rage, and until I awakened from the terrible trance of fury that held me prisoner, I could not be calm, content or genuinely free.

This is a problem all too common for black people today. And yet, it is difficult for many of us to recognize our rage as a problem, because we are taught daily that it is appropriate, and even a good thing, a sort of badge of authentic blackness. Think of Louis Farrakhan, Maxine Waters, Al Sharpton, Jesse Jackson, Kweisi Mfume, Danny Bakewell, the assortment of privileged blacks in Congress, universities and media—these are some of the most angry people in America, and yet they are widely regarded as the gatekeepers of black progress, the true advocates for black interests.

It is against the crippling resentment of their politics and psychology that I write. My own experience has emphatically taught me that the emotions of rage and bitterness don't help people overcome their problems, they only make those problems worse.

In the pages that follow, I will show how the culturally contentious areas of race, gender relations, abortion, education and immigration have been further complicated by our general politics of acrimony and animosity, and how, by better understanding the personally and socially corrosive consequences such attitudes bring, we as individuals and as a political culture can better function.

Chapter Two

THE PROBLEM WITH RACE

I cannot believe you are talking like this! You can't talk about black people like this! You're not really black, you're a white man in a black man's body! Stop blaming the victim!
—An irate caller to a talkradio program on which Jesse Peterson was a guest, berating him for his views.

As my story—the story of a common black American—shows, blacks have suffered much in the history of this country. From the actual deprivations of slavery and Jim Crow, to the residual effects of those tragedies in the black psyche and the black family, the depth of black suffering has been unique. Indeed, of all the groups in America vying for victimhood, it is only black Americans who can legitimately make the claim that in American history they have been systematically and continuously persecuted.

The question then, facing every black person in this country is, "What are you going to do about the wrongs of the past, how will you react now to what happened then?" Far too many black "leaders" urge us to incorporate the sins of the past into our consciousness today, and manifest today the anger that was warranted then. They do this because they have found great social and political capital in anger. If more blacks are angry, they strengthen their position as the hostile voices of black consciousness and expression.

So, of course, in order to lend credence to this psychology of rage which they want to imprint on contemporary black Americans, they shamelessly exaggerate about the extent of racism today. Millionaire rapper Ice Cube is a typical example of this, saying in a 1991 press conference, "The American Dream isn't for blacks. Blacks who [still believe in that dream] are kidding themselves. There's only room in that dream for a few Blacks."[1]

Unfortunately, the examples of black Americans—encouraged by their advocates—exaggerating about racism could be multiplied many times. Johnnie Cochran, Jr. famously said "Race plays a part of everything in America"; former Illinois senator Carol Mosely Braun called conservative columnist George Will a Klansman for criticizing her during her 1998 Senate re-election campaign; Spike Lee seriously wondered if AIDS was created by whites to destroy blacks, and on and on. The siege mentality black leadership has created in the consciousness of many black Americans has led them to accept the assumption of rampant, systematic, anti-black racism in America.

I believe that a more accurate, reasonable, and practically helpful position for black people to adopt is what I call "Pro-American Individualism." This is the land of freedom and innovation which provides people with opportunity for social and economic advancement unrivaled anywhere on the globe. If people adopt the values that make for personal success—hard work, careful spending of money, sustained effort, delayed gratification—and keep themselves psychologically healthy by rejecting rage and resentment as the controlling attitudes of their lives, they will do well. If you want to succeed in this country, and you're willing to work hard, you will. I think the record of American history verifies this. As individuals, we control our own destinies in this country more than anyone else does anywhere else on the planet. Upward mobility can be a reality for anyone willing to adopt the personal habits that make for success.

As much as some people hate to admit it, and as angry as it makes many black people, *the undeniable fact is that the greatest enemies to black progress today are within the black community itself, not in American society at large.* As black people, we must recognize that our real battle is with ourselves, not with society. It is not racism but the civil rights establishment, with its victim-centered mentality and irrational fury at white America that mentally cripples blacks, teaching them to find the means of success outside of themselves in government programs, and urging them to find the origin of their greatest problems in white society.

But the politically-incorrect truth is that racism today is a state of mind, more than a social reality. Oh yes, it exists, and the news media is always quick to highlight examples of anti-black racial hostility, but it is not the all-powerful, institutional beast so many say it is. But once people believe racism is their main problem, they become subject to that idea, and it prevents them from progressing.

I remember one young black boy I counseled, telling me over and over how much it bothered him that the members of another basketball team against which he was competing had called him a "Nigger." I told him to forget about it and concentrate on his game, but he could not get past it. So I said "Did they get extra points for calling you that?" "Did they get to shoot foul shots for calling you that?" "Did they get to shoot 3-pointers from beneath the basket for calling you that?" He sheepishly answered "No," and I told him to try his hardest, because those boys were accomplishing nothing for themselves by talking like that, and could only hurt him if he allowed them to. I said, "Your future is in your hands, not theirs, so don't waste energy thinking about those fools." I think he got the message.

But for black Americans as a whole, we still have not understood how we should regard ourselves at this point in time. The tragedy of this moment is hard to overemphasize. Just as all significant barriers to black progress have fallen away, it is as though black people have folded their arms in contempt and refused to move forward.

While serious economic gains have been made by many, and there is a solid black middle class, there are still about a third of black Americans mired in poverty and despair, paralyzed by their anger and the rhetoric of hopelessness relentlessly broadcast to them by their supposed "leaders." If only they had adopted the wisdom of Abraham Lincoln who once said, "I am less interested in who my grandfather was than in what his grandson will be," they would be mentally equipped to walk through the open door that history and the genius of the American experiment have provided.

How then did we get to this point, where so many black Americans are paralyzed by racial obsession, racial groupthink, and racial rage? And what is the way out? To these questions we now turn.

Race Consciousness

One of the most constant features of world history has been racism. Whether from one ethnically homogenous nation toward another, or from one particular ethnicity toward another within an ethnically heterogeneous nation, people of all races have, at one time or another, been guilty of racism. This underlines the truth that racism is a product of universal human nature, not a property of one group of people alone. Racists come in all colors and creeds. That is why the Hebrew Bible makes clear that the hardest thing in life for human beings to do is to love the stranger. We are naturally suspicious of those who do not look like us. Only by coming to know one another, do we break through the stereotypes and see each other as human beings first, and members of a given race second, if at all.

I'm reminded of another young black man I counseled. I'll call him Tyrone. He was bright and talented in many ways, but was absolutely full of rage. He had come from a difficult family background; his father left him, his mother and two brothers, when he was a baby. The resentment he felt at his father and mother expressed itself in his life as rage at white people, whom he had learned from black peers and neighbors to blame for his troubles. He refused to try hard at low wage jobs, and as a result never progressed. He repeated to me the usual lines one hears in black communities about white people being "devils" and "racist thieves." When I asked him if he knew any white people personally, he said "no." I introduced him to a couple of young white men I was also counseling, and over time he became friends with them, and came to trust them.

When I talked with him again a few months later, I asked him
how he felt about white people. He was still suspicious of them,
but now he was ready to make judgments about them on an
individual basis, rather than only as a group. He stopped speaking of "white people," and instead spoke of "white individuals."
His vision had broken through the prism of his own ethnicity,
and he was able to see others as persons, not colors.

Tyrone's initial color-coded thinking is what the rampant race-
consciousness of America has engendered. It has taught minorities to derive their personal identity from their race, instead of
their character; to think of themselves as a color first, and not a
person. Of course, this is ironic given that the emphasis on race
is what the original civil rights movement fought to overcome.
Ethicist Dennis Prager has helpfully noted the origin of so much
of our racial obsession, and why it is so wrong:

> With the collapse of a strong identity as American and/or as
> Christian/Jew/Other Religion, a new generation of Americans
> seeks its identity in race and ethnicity, i. e., in blood, not values.
> This affirmation of race and ethnicity as exemplified by the many
> racial and ethnic clubs at American public high schools and the
> race-ethnicity-based dormitories at colleges throughout America
> was deemed racist and primitive when I was a student. Today, it
> is deemed progressive. The change, an entirely regressive one,
> should make those who believe that social change is always good
> or that societies inevitably progress take heed.[2]

Additionally, for blacks, race consciousness has grown because
there is now social and political benefit to be had by emphasizing one's blackness: It's "cool," you can get preferential treatment in many areas (college admission, government work, corporate America), and you are often treated deferentially by the
larger culture.

But the psychological and material rewards of race come at
too heavy a price. One such cost is the surrendering of one's individuality to be a part of a group. When group identity replaces
individual identity, one must adopt the patterns of opinion man-

dated by the group, or be excommunicated by the group. That is why we see so much ideological conformity in black America. From mindless loyalty to the Democratic party to allegiance to professional race workers like Jesse Jackson, it is considered "un-black" to dissent from agreeing with such forces.

This has been driven home very powerfully recently by the solid, uncritical black support for President Clinton, even in the face of his reprehensible, reckless, and clearly illegal behavior. The gulf in black/white opinion regarding Bill Clinton, follow-ing his sexual trysts with Monica Lewinsky and his lies about that affair, was remarkable. To the question, "Do you have a fa-vorable opinion of Bill Clinton?" we get, for whites, 42% favor-able, 47% unfavorable. But for blacks, we get 82% favorable, 4% unfavorable. And to the question, "Do you believe that Bill Clinton shares the moral values most Americans try to live by?" whites say yes 29%, no 66%, but blacks say yes 71%, no 25%.[3] Black icon Toni Morrison went so far as to famously call the immoral Clinton "our first black president." This celebrity and political support for President Clinton and liberalism generally undermines the vitality of the black community by urging us to simply "get in line" and follow our racial leaders, rather than give expression to our own personal opinions, which may be differ-ent. Sadly, too many black Americans willingly conform their minds and obey. A more individualist view is presented by Justice Clarence Thomas, who said in another context: "I...refuse to have my ideas assigned to me as though I was an intellectual slave because I'm black."[4]

Another significant cost associated with race-consciousness is the anger it necessitates. To be a member of a racial group is to always be on guard against slights and insults. One must culti-vate a super-sensitivity to racism, and react with great fury when-ever one perceives it. An "us-against-them" mentality results, and one's individuality begins to recede behind a wall of racial anger and personal hostility that is poisonous to the person. Happiness and anger cannot coincide, and the person infected with race consciousness is inevitably going to harbor hostility against those

who he thinks have not treated his group with sufficient deference and respect.

We find in black America both of these baleful effects of race
consciousness: ideological conformity and racial rage. But in my
experience, it is the latter, racial rage, that has done the most to
damage black people. It has robbed them of a sense of personal
peace, making them vulnerable to manipulation by self-appointed
black leaders, seducing them into the perversely satisfying immorality of racial hatred.

Black Rage

The racial anger of black America obviously has its origins in the
mistreatments of the past. But that anger did not fade away as
past injustices were righted; instead, ironically, it only grew, fomented by a self-interested class of race workers, and a white
liberal elite in media and academe only too willing to parrot politically-correct slogans about race, so that they would not be called
"racist."[5] And, as I will discuss later—and have already suggested—
black rage is also a manifestation of resentment and dissatisfac-
tion with parents, particularly fathers.

Black rage is generally accepted in this country as the appropriate attitude for black people to have. So much so, that its reality is seldom openly recognized and acknowledged.[6] Tragically,
in my view, many black Americans are angry at white people,
angry at Jewish people, angry at black conservatives, and angry
at America.[7] Consider this roll-call of culturally-approved black
rage:

• Black commentator Karen Grigsby Bates hysterically as-
sails white senators as racists for considering the impeachment
of President Bill Clinton. Writing on the op-ed page of the *Los
Angeles Times* she says, "[W]henever I hear Trent Lott speak, I
immediately think of nooses decorating trees. Big trees, with black
bodies swinging from the business end of the nooses....Strom
Thurmond natters on, and, I just see the Old South: Panama-

wearing, sharecropper-cheating, dismissive and condescending."[8]

• Emphatic cheers erupt at a filled-to-capacity Madison Square Garden, during a rally held by the Nation of Islam, when a speaker merely mentions the name of Colin Ferguson—the Long Island commuter train gunman who murdered several people out of anger at whites and, in his words, "Uncle Tom Negroes." After the shooting, a *National Law Journal* survey shows that 68% of blacks believe that white racism caused Ferguson to kill.[9] A black professor at New York University calls Ferguson a "hero," and says he knows colleagues who are admiringly placing Ferguson's picture on their walls, next to Malcolm X.[10]

• Upon O. J. Simpson's acquittal in his 1994 criminal trial, black students at a Howard University auditorium, gathering to watch the verdict, cheer ecstatically.

• A celebrated black author calls the 1992 Los Angeles riots, in which more than 50 people were murdered, "a display of justified social rage."[11] Black economist Julianne Malveaux declares, "Racism is as American as the Constitution," and attributes the L. A. riots to ineffective affirmative action programs and declining urban aid.[12]

• In Brooklyn in 1991, after an elderly Hassidic Jewish man kills a black child in an auto accident, black residents take to the streets yelling, "Heil Hitler!" and "Zionazi!" When they come upon Australian rabbinic student Yankel Rosenbaum, someone in the mob yells "Get the Jew!" Rosenbaum is attacked, and stabbed to death. Lemrick Nelson, a young black man, is charged with the crime, but acquitted by a predominantly black jury. This, even though police find Nelson near the scene with a bloody knife in his possession; the blood on the knife is verified by DNA analysis to be Rosenbaum's; Nelson is identified by the dying Rosenbaum as his attacker, and Nelson confesses to the murder. After the verdict the black jury members party with Nelson's attorney. As Eric Breindel wrote of the events at the time, "For Hassidic Jews New York City today is a lot like the Jim Crow south was for blacks themselves 30 years ago. Justice is all but unattainable."[13]

• Georgia congresswoman Cynthia McKinney denounces the Supreme Court decision forbidding racial gerrymandered congressional districts as racist, and white voters as race-based. Her newly drawn district is a majority white district, yet, when these voters return her to Congress in the 1996 election, she complains that her victory will be used by opponents of affirmative action to assert that whites are not racist.[14]

Indeed, writer Ellis Cose notes that middle class blacks have "deeply repressed rage," and are as pessimistic about this country and their life chances as the seriously poor.[15]

Why is black rage such a prominent feature of black life? Racial anger has a special power over the human psyche. It gives one the illusion of power and retribution, and makes one feel as though one is effectively fighting back against a perceived offense. Further, like all anger, it feeds on itself, and only grows. It is self-sustaining, and can lead its true believers literally anywhere, physically or morally. Kwame Ture, the former Stokley Carmichael, originator of the "black power" phrase, ended up moving to Africa after his tenure in America as angry student radical par excellence. There, in Africa, he died of prostate cancer in 1998, still furious at a great many people and institutions.[16] At his funeral, a large banner hung over the dais, reading "The CIA gave me cancer. Kwame Ture."[17]

And sometimes race-based anger just leads to lies. Al Sharpton, Alton Maddox Jr., and C. Vernon Mason, were found by a racially mixed jury to have defamed white prosecutor Steven Pagones in the infamous Tawana Brawley case in New York City, when they accused Pagones of participating in the rape of Brawley. Afterward Pagones sensibly commented, "They [Sharpton, Maddox, Mason] hurt race relations. We have enough problems in society, we don't need people like Mason, Maddox and Sharpton screaming out false allegations and creating further hatred."[18] But to Brawley's defenders, the truth of her account of rape was not the main point, rather, the expression of their racial rage was what really mattered. And Pagones was the innocent person they used to voice that hostility.

So black anger is dangerous in many ways. It is self-destructive, it can lead to lies and hysteria, and it can also lead to naked violence. Black anger is, particularly in youth, a powder keg waiting to explode.

For example, recently, in a small town in Pennsylvania, a 39-year-old white woman named Valerie Johnson was walking down a street with her three-year-old son. They passed by two black male teenagers whose conversation was filled with use of the word "nigger." Johnson's toddler innocently repeated the word he had heard them say. Enraged, one of the black teens hit Valerie Johnson in the head. She apologized for her son's mistake, then went home and called the police. Later that same day, Ms. Johnson and her child were walking elsewhere in the town, when the same two black teens, plus one other young black male, attacked her, throwing her to the ground and violently kicking her, as her child stood by screaming. Ms. Johnson was rushed to the hospital. She died three days later.[19]

While, as I've noted, the inflammatory rhetoric of racial provocateurs is a major cause of black rage today, there is also a family factor at work. In my own life, the anger and fury I carried around with me everywhere I went—which, for many years, I directed at white people—was primarily the product of being abandoned by my father. I hated and resented him for leaving me; I hated and resented my mother for hating him; and I hated and resented both of them together for not succeeding as a family. It was my fragmented and troubled family life that was the basic source of my hostility and discontent. As a young man, I translated that into racial rage because that gave me a feeling—however false—of self-control and power. By hating white people and being angry at America, I avoided the pain of facing my resentment of my parents, and my hurtful awareness of how they failed me. I missed not having a father to love me and nurture me into manhood. In his place, I accepted hostility toward others, particularly whites—those who my community had taught me were the origin of my suffering as a black man in America.

It is disconcerting but true: black leaders exploit the family problems of black people, especially black people's poor relations with their fathers. Family pain in the backgrounds of many black people is the foundation, the real fuel for power, for race men. They use blacks' internal resentment of their parents, particularly their fathers, to help generate anger at white people and American culture. That's why you don't see a massive, overwhelming effort on the part of black leaders to rescue the institution of black fatherhood, which—with about 70% of black births out-of-wedlock—is plainly nearing extinction. Civil rights groups don't emphasize the centrality of the family to black progress, but rather the value of government initiatives and group identity. Too much of a focus on the black family and its restoration would in time reduce the personal anger of many blacks, and thus undercut the social influence of the race industry. So, we black Americans continue along in this racial mess, obeying our *de facto* spokesmen, being angry at white people, and neglecting our own homes.

But this is a path doomed to self-destruction and permanent unhappiness. Rage, hostility, anger, fury, resentment, etc., never lead to social mobility or personal peace. Instead, they inculcate within oneself a deeply rooted victim identity. Yet, understanding oneself to be a part of a ruthlessly victimized group only gives one company in misery, it doesn't solve any real problems, or lead to any real happiness. Dennis Prager explains why the victim mentality is only a prescription for discontent:

> [T]oday some people continue to view themselves as victims because of the *historical* suffering of their group and because it is easy and comforting to do so. And this renders happiness virtually impossible. First…perceiving yourself as a victim makes you unhappy. Second, it makes you permanently angry, which further guarantees unhappiness. Third, it enables you to avoid confronting whatever it is that is really making you unhappy.[20]

The Race Hustlers

Make no mistake, the race industry in this country is a tremendously profitable business. It is financed largely by government grants and liberal foundations. For example, the Ford Foundation gives away an average of more than $1 million a day, virtually never to conservative causes. They are, on the other hand, a regular supporter of the NAACP, even after that organization demonstrated terrible stewardship of its budget, paying hundreds of thousands of dollars out in sexual harassment settlements.

But because the race card is such an effective tool, and because government bodies, foundations, and corporations desperately want to avoid being called "racists," civil rights groups with undistinguished records of contemporary accomplishment find it easy to raise money by threatening to use the "R" word. For example, at the 1998 NAACP convention, Kweisi Mfume declared "race and skin color still dominates [sic] every aspect of American life, at home and abroad." The next day Vice President Al Gore told the convention that the Small Business Administration would provide $1.4 billion in loans for black-owned businesses over the next two years. Gore said the NAACP would act as liaison to black businessmen.[21] Similarly, a group of black concert promoters, specializing in rap and hip-hop acts, sued some of the music industry's top talent agencies for $700 million, claiming that racial discrimination against them has prevented them for booking major concerts.[22] No word yet on the amount of a settlement. And black farmers successfully sued the United States government, arguing racist agricultural policies. They won several million dollars.

Such racial shakedowns are common. But they are based on a false view of American life as racist. The fact is most blacks have made tremendous progress since World War II, because once legal fairness was instituted, they showed that they are just as capable as anyone else of supporting themselves. Consider these seldom repeated facts of black accomplishment:

• Black citizens earning $50,000 a year or more are the fastest growing income group in America.[23]

• Since the 1960's, the percentage of wealthy black Americans has more than doubled.[24]

• Thomas Sowell asserts that by the late 1960's, black men

from families with a library card, magazines and other literature in the home reached high-level occupations as often as white males of similar backgrounds.[25]

• In families where both parents are college educated and both parents work, black families tend to make more than white families. This is the case in all parts of the United States, for families of all ages.[26]

• From 1982 to 1987, the number of companies owned by blacks increased by a third, and their gross incomes more than doubled. During this same period, non-black owned businesses increased by only 14%.[27]

• The number of black-owned enterprises nearly doubled during the last decade—five times the rate of new business creation for the country as a whole.[28]

• Among black, white, and Hispanic Americans with the same age and IQ, annual earnings are comparable, within $1,000 of each other.[29]

• In 1985, 8% of college students, aged 18-24, were black. By 1995, the percentage was 11%, just under the 12.5% that would be parity. The 1987 data also showed that the percentage of black high school graduates in the cohort aged 25-29 equals 86% for blacks, 87% for whites. Twenty-three percent of whites aged 25-29 held college degrees in 1987, compared to 11% for blacks. But just ten years later, 29% for whites, 14% for blacks.[30]

This certainly does not sound like the description of a racist nation that hates black people.[31] And it hardly fits the rhetoric of black leaders which portrays black people all over America as constantly shut out of the job market, defamed in media, and harassed by the police. As William Raspberrry put it, "Much of black leadership would rather deny racial progress than claim credit for it, apparently finding more political power in highlighting problems rather than in solving them."[32]

So the hypocrisy of conventional black leadership comes into clear focus. While they close their eyes to black progress, they will cry "Racism!" with every leaf that falls, and take great umbrage at the slightest racial slip—Al Campanis on *Nightline* opining on why blacks aren't great swimmers, Ross Perot referring to his NAACP audience as "you people," a city employee publicly using the word "niggardly," even though its meaning is unrelated to the racial epithet it resembles.

Compounding this dereliction, mainstream black advocacy groups are nearly completely silent about atrocities committed against black people by other blacks, and the anguish that results.[33] For example:

• Today, in Sudan and Mauritania, black men, women and children are routinely sold into slavery, yet American civil rights organizations are utterly silent about it.[34]

• Nearly 70% of black children in America are born out of wedlock. This is the most basic social problem facing blacks, as it leads to kids being raised without fathers, which causes everything from drug use to violent criminality to sexual promiscuity. But the Urban League, NAACP, SCLC, and other groups pay only lip service to this problem. They simply will not address the moral dysfunction underlying it.

• A CDC report released in 1998 showed that the suicide rate for young black males aged 10-19 increased 114% since 1980. White youth are still more likely to take their own life, but the gap is dramatically narrowing. In 1980 the suicide rate for young whites was 157% greater than it was for young blacks, but today the rate is only 42% greater.[35] Should not groups purporting to represent the interests of black Americans be addressing this problem?

• Black women are 8 times more likely to get HIV than are white women, and 3 times more likely than Hispanic women. Nationwide, almost half of all HIV positive women are black.[36] Shouldn't black leaders teach against sex outside of marriage? Instead, there are prominent black churches in Los Angeles and accross America that are actually willing suppliers of condoms to sexually active people.

• According to one 1996 study in California, 39% of black men in their 20s in that state were either on probation, in jail or on parole.[37] Another study found that 33% of all California state prisoners are black, even though only 7.5% of California's population is black.[38] Nationwide, a study by a liberal research group, the Sentencing Project, found that more than 30% of black men in their 20s were touched by the penal system.[39] Murder is the leading cause of death for black men between the ages of 15 and 34, and these murders are nearly always committed by other blacks. It doesn't take a genius to see that young black men have a problem with crime. They are inflicting tremendous misery on their own black communities, and on our country as a whole.

Yet instead of engaging the failure of black churches to affect the morality of black youth, and rather than facing the reality that many black communities are living in abject *moral* poverty, civil rights groups choose to lobby companies like Denny's and Texaco for more minority preferences, and protest the lack of black coaches in the NBA and NFL. Indeed, in a stunning display of their complete unwillingness to confront the *moral and spiritual problems* in the black community, the NAACP recently announced its intention to sue handgun manufacturers, distributors and importers, thinking this will decrease the presence of guns in black communities, and stem the flood of black-on-black violence.[40]

Why then does the civil rights establishment avoid addressing the real problems causing black suffering? Because deep down, they are more angry at white people than they are in love with black people. Their deepest agenda is one of agitation and accusation against white America, not aid and comfort to black America. This is a provocative claim in the eyes of many, but any serious observer of the rhetoric and politics of these groups can only conclude that they are motivated by anger at America more than desire for black uplift. The liberal agenda they pursue is statist and premised on class resentment, it stifles black entrepreneurship, and it places as the main engine of black progress the civil rights establishment itself, rather than individual black people succeeding on their own through hard work and discipline. Black leaders have a professional interest in ensuring that poor blacks continue to lead a degenerate life, so they will be subject to them. Black leaders' livelihoods depend on being the saviors of the "have-nots" and the "victims" of American racism. They cannot permit blacks' problems truly to be solved, because then they themselves, as institutions, would become unnecessary. The race industry, like any bureaucracy, is self-perpetuating and self-protecting. If new problems need to be manufactured to justify their organizations' existence or budget, they will invent the problems.

Black Racism

While there is much talk about freedom of speech in our culture, the fact is that some topics are absolutely off limits for anyone who wants to be regarded as "enlightened" and "in-touch." Black racism, perhaps more than any other topic, is such a subject. There is nothing less than a *code of silence* in the black community about black racism. Black leaders and many common black citizens believe that if blacks openly confront this reality of black life, blacks' social and political authority will be impaired, since blacks will not be seen so much as innocent victims, but rather as victimizers. Therefore, blacks who speak out against black racism are criticized very harshly—and so are their families.

I have experienced black racism regularly. I've been called "nigger," "Uncle Tom," "Sellout," and "bought" by white people. My life itself has been threatened by black people afraid of my criticisms of black racism. The truth is, as an adult, I've experienced more racism from other black people than I have from white people. I've been hated because, as a black man, I love America, and am reluctant to criticize it. Since blacks are taught by their leaders and communities to hate whites and be angry at the United States, anything except the typical condemnations of whites and this country is offensive to them.

In my opinion, black-on-black racism is the worst kind of racism. The hatred is intense. You become a total outcast. Witness the treatment accorded Supreme Court Justice Clarence Thomas, during his tenure on the bench and the public spotlight generally. San Francisco mayor Willie Brown's comments to the Association of Black Sociologists are emblematic of the hateful attitude most black people—at the behest of their "leaders"—have adopted towards black conservatives like Clarence Thomas: "[Clarence Thomas] must not be allowed any comfort from any of us," Brown said, "He should be reduced to talking to only white conservatives. He must be shut out."[41] As black dissident Larry Elder put it, "Black anger is, today, as strong as a force of nature. It is a powerful, unpleasant thing to have directed at you."[42] That is what awaits any black person who blows the whistle on black racism. And if you're white and try it, you'll certainly be branded a "racist devil" immediately. But it has been my experience that white people, including white conservatives, rarely speak out about black racism.[43] They're just too intimidated.

Anyone who doubts the reality of black racism should consider these many shameful events:

• Willie Brown, now mayor of San Francisco, once referred to his former colleagues in the California legislature as "white boys," and called Clarence Thomas a "shill for racism," because of his opinions.[44]

• Joel Lee, a Korean-American in Baltimore, was shot in the head for no apparent reason, by a young black man who walked up to him, pointed the gun at him, and fired into his head, point blank. Four witnesses saw the killing, two others said the suspect confessed to them, and the suspect's uncle told police that his nephew admitted doing the murder, and bragged about it, saying he hated Koreans, and that was the sole reason he did it. This black suspect was acquitted by a jury that said the prosecution's six witnesses all lacked credibility. The jury had 11 black people on it. After serving jail time on an unrelated drug charge, this suspect was freed back into the black community.[45]

• Black Muslim Khalid Muhammad called Rudolf Giuliani, mayor of New York, "an ordinary cracker," and a "devil."[46]

• At a black college, Khalid Muhammad told a throng of cheering black students, referring to white people living in South Africa, "If the white man won't get out of town by sundown, we kill everything white in South Africa. We kill the women, we kill the children, we kill the babies.... Kill the blind, kill the crippled, and when you get through killing them all, go to the graveyard, dig up the grave, and kill them again."[47] New York state senator David Paterson pointed out the fruitlessness of Khalid Muhammad's hate: "How does denying that there was a Holocaust get black kids job opportunities? How does advocating the killing of South African whites help black kids to get an education?"[48]

• Rapper and author Sister Souljah, expressed her hatred of white people by saying they have a "low-down dirty nature."[49] If a white celebrity said that about black people, she would never be publically heard from again. Ever.

• Black ethnocentrism is so strong that more white families are ready to adopt black kids than are black families ready to adopt white kids.[50] As writer Jim Sleeper pointed out, the National Association of Black Social Workers (NABSW) actively prevents whites from adopting black kids. The NABSW has adopted regulations that require abandoned black infants be left to languish in hospitals in case other black families can be found to adopt them, rather than allow the babies to go to a white family that wants them and is ready to adopt them. Sleeper says, "Apparently white love is as threatening as white hate to those who would rather treat a race as a 'family' than respect individuals' cross-racial moral choices."[51] The NABSW policy is racialism over humanism. To them, simply put, race is more important than human feelings and family love. Race *uber alles*, "Race above all," should be their motto. It is a purely racist policy, but our culture accepts it, because it is black racism.

• After the tragic murder of her son Ennis, Camille Cosby blamed the whole nation, not just the killer, writing, "I believe America taught our son's killer to hate African-Americans."[52]

• Marion Barry once said a majority white city council in Washington, D. C., would be bad for the district's majority black population (63%), because when it comes to making laws, blacks and whites are different "in terms of culture, in terms of philosophy."[53] Such a comment from a white person would immediately result in their vigorous condemnation.

• Signithia Fordham, a black sociologist, claimed high levels of black support for President Clinton following his admission of the Lewinsky affair was due to blacks' surety of the fact that everyone else who might be president may be a racist. She said, "We are so afraid of what might come after him if he leaves. It's not that African-Americans are overlooking his breach in appropriate behavior, but we are making a practical and political decision that is in our best interests. We say this president is the best of the evils that could happen to us and the country."[54]

• One black South African writer who emigrated to the U. S. said he saw blacks saying the same things about whites here that whites did about blacks there. Black students told him they found "satisfaction" in hating white people.[55]

• During the 1992 Los Angeles riots, non-blacks were beaten on sight by black mobs. One Hispanic woman was seized upon by a group, after someone in the group saw her, and shouted, "Get her. She's not a sister!" After the riots a black gang member told Ted Koppell, "everybody that came through [my neighborhood] that was not black was in trouble."[56]

• Nathan McCall, a black author and reporter for the *Washington Post,* told of his own hatred of white people. Describing an incident in which he and a group of other young blacks attacked a young white who rode through their neighborhood on a bicycle, McCall wrote: "We all took off after him. We caught him and knocked him off the bike. He fell to the ground and it was all over. We were on him. We stomped and kicked him. My partners kicked him in the head and face and watched the blood gush from his mouth. I kicked him in the stomach and nuts." As he beat him, McCall, explained, "I felt better." Believing this was racial revenge, McCall says he thought to himself, "This is for all the times you followed me round in stores. And this is for the times you treated me like a nigger. And this is for general principle—just 'cause you white."[57]

• Deep down, even black people know that many of them have feelings of contempt and hatred for whites. For example, during O.J. Simpson's criminal trial for murder, prior to a visit by jurors to Simpson's house to inspect the scene, Simpson's lawyer, Johnnie Cochran, Jr., had all Simpson's pictures of his white girl-friends removed because those photos were sure to anger the many black women on the jury. They were replaced by pictures of black people, pictures which had been enlarged at Kinko's and nicely framed.[58] Similarly, during the Los Angeles riots of 1992, black shop owners spray-painted the declaration "Black-owned" on their storefronts, knowing that stores owned by Koreans or other non-blacks would be torched by the black rioters.

• Some black ministers tolerate black racial hatred. After one white man using a phone booth was confronted in a mixed-race New York City neighborhood and told by a pair of black men "You don't belong here," he was shot and killed. In response to this racist hate murder, a prominent black minister, who had con-demned the infamous Bensonhurst case of a black youth being murdered by young white racists, said "I don't know if [the mur-der of the white man is] racism as I define it. There's a difference between racism and revenge."[59]

Beyond these particular examples, as horrifying as they are, the racist attitudes of many black people are further exemplified in overall national crime statistics:

• More than 90% of interracial crime victims are white.[60]

• Blacks are responsible for 50 times more violent racial crimes than are whites,[61] and are nearly 50 times more likely to perpe-trate violent crimes against whites, than whites are against blacks.[62]

• Blacks murder whites at 18 times the rate that whites mur-der blacks.[63]

• A black man is 64 times more likely to rape a white woman than a white man is to rape a black woman. Even the very liberal author Andrew Hacker admits that blacks rape whites far more frequently than the reverse. In fact, rape has become a predomi-nately black male crime.[64]

The unavoidable conclusion is this: black politicians' and ra-cial spokesmen's continual drumbeat about the racism surrounding black people, and the bigotry of white people thwarting blacks' best efforts, causes in many blacks—particularly black youth—a hatred of whites. It's no more complicated than that. The politically-correct script of American social life, which features meanspirited white oppressors and innocent black victims, has signaled to black youth, and a good many older black people, that it's perfectly understandable, and even appropriate, to hate white people, to blame them for black suffering, and to freely, even violently, express contempt for them.

Black racism is one of the ugliest realities in our culture, and, the truth is, until more people start exposing it and condemning it, we blacks as a race cannot heal ourselves of this sinful attitude, and reach a place of personal peace. The solution to our race problem is that we must begin to look at ourselves as individuals first. When we conduct self-examination, engage in self-inventory, and come to understand ourselves, we will begin to overcome our own anger, which is the necessary first step to personal recovery and happiness.

But most blacks are prevented from this self-examination and self-criticism, because they don't think for themselves as individuals first; they instead willingly accept the opinions they know they are supposed to have as racial victims. They embrace the attitudes cued to them by black politicians and racial professionals.

But when you see yourself as an individual first, you are freed to think for yourself, and you become internally self-sufficient. You start to break free from the bonds of racial conformity, and you start to see the good and bad in everyone, irrespective of their color. You start to be less angry, and as you let go of anger you are empowered to love God, your family, and your country.

So then we have this paradox: the solution to America's race problem—a problem analyzed and discussed for decades by armies of sociologists, politicians and activists—is internal, not external. It is inward, not outward; personal, not social; individual, not political.

Let me conclude by presenting five quotations from very well-regarded scholars and commentators which state as clearly as possible the reality blacks face in this country today. Please, listen carefully to this wisdom, because in its embrace is authentic freedom:

• Cal Thomas: "The impediment to greater black progress is not racial discrimination. It is family breakdown. In every category—from out-of-wedlock births and fatherless homes, to the percentage of young males in prison and victims or perpetrators of violent crimes—blacks are disproportionately affected because it is their racial group that suffers most from broken or never-formed two-parent homes."[65]

• Walter Williams: "The major problems that stand in the way of broader [black] advancement will be solved only when blacks finally recognize that our destinies finally lie in our hands and only we can solve what are essentially black problems—not Washington, politicians and the intellectual elite."[66]

• Ward Connerly: "It is high time those who are obsessed with color develop a little colorblindness. We have to stop dwelling on past injustices like slavery and segregation. And we have to accept this fact: We can't use race to get beyond race."[67]

• Shelby Steele: "[I]t is time for those who seek identity and power through grievance groups to fashion identities apart from grievance, to grant themselves the widest range of freedom, and to assume responsibility for that freedom."[68]

• Dinesh D'Souza: "One thing is clear: Racism is no longer the main problem facing blacks or any other group in America today. Even if racism were to disappear overnight, this would do nothing to improve black test scores, increase black entrepreneurship, strengthen black families, or reduce black-on-black crime. These problems have taken on a cultural existence of their own and need to be confronted in their own terms."[69]

Chapter Three

THE PROBLEM WITH MEN AND WOMEN

> You really bug me! The only differences between men and women
> are the differences society makes. I'm really just like you. And
> anybody who denies that is wrong, wrong, wrong!!
> > —*A white female feminist, arguing with Jesse during*
> > *a Q and A session following a campus debate.*

In few spheres of American life is there as much confusion as
there is in the area of men and women, and their relationships
together. Psychologist John Gray has capitalized on this pathetic
phenomenon, making his *Men Are from Mars, Women Are from
Venus* bestselling books and seminars into a small industry.

We are in nothing less than a crisis of sexual self-understand-
ing. We wonder who we are and what we should be, even as we
tell ourselves that the "old morality" of Judeo-Christian absolutes
has no relevance today.

But this crisis of personal relationships is symptomatic of our
larger cultural devolution. Today, about 44% of all first births are
to unmarried women. Since 1960, the divorce rate has more than
doubled, the rate of out-of-wedlock births has increased six-fold,
and the rate at which young men and women take their own
lives has tripled.[1] From the highest office in the land to the dysfunctional displays of the *Jerry Springer Show* (the two venues
are bearing an increasing likeness), people are failing to keep their
commitments to one another, and sexual irresponsibility is destroying lives.

In my view we need to return to the standards of the past to
solve the interpersonal problems and confusions of today. People

now are seeking deep wisdom for living, and that is to be found only in the tried and true traditions of yesterday, not the trends of today. I think the evident hunger for understanding each other that men and women are displaying, plus the obvious downward spiral of social morality, proves that we need to radically re-think prevailing views of men and women.

Presently, under the auspices of contemporary feminism, it is generally believed that mothers and fathers are interchangeable in their parental roles, that all men and women are basically the same, and that sex is a casual matter between consenting adults. Each of these ideas significantly contributes to the inability of men and women to understand themselves, and get along with one another. Let us, then, look at these destructive notions in turn.

The Centrality of Fatherhood

Before any social repair can begin, we have to recognize the nature of our problems. And the fact is, today, fatherlessness is our most urgent social dysfunction. From out of wedlock births, to violence among boys, to rape and abuse of women, to drug use and poor school performance, most social pathologies can be traced to today's epidemic fatherlessness. Every night, fully 40% of American children go to bed in homes in which their fathers do not live.[2] The psychological effects on children, male and female, of this alienation from their fathers is impossible to measure, but common sense dictates that it must be profound.

And yet, fatherlessness continues to proliferate, because contemporary liberalism has dismissed its seriousness in an effort to sexually homogenize society. Thus, it is widely believed in our country today, that mothers and fathers are duplicates of one another, that they are redundant, and that all a woman really needs from a man is his income to successfully raise "her" children. This is the nonsense that the triumph of feminism has given us.

But to me, it is self-evident that men and women, as fathers and mothers, each have unique gifts they can give their children. Every child has a natural right to a mother and a father, and to the contributions toward his well-being that each parent can uniquely make. Where a mother is nurturing, a father is challenging; where a mother is compassionate and emotionally indulgent, a father is fairly strict and stern; where a mother dotes, a father prods. This is more than a sort of parental good-cop/bad-cop routine, it is the natural order of the family, one that corresponds to the general character and dispositions of psychologically healthy women and men.

The different ways mothers and fathers tend to react to their children prove that they each have something indispensable to give to them. If a young boy is trying to climb a tree and he falls, modestly injuring himself, his mother will come to him, upset, and say, "Oh honey, are you all right? You're not climbing any more trees!" The mother's powerful regard for her child's safety causes her to react this way. Of course, the boy will almost certainly continue to climb trees anyway.

But if after the boy falls, his father comes to him, his father will say, "Are you all right? *Here, let me show you how to climb that tree.*" A father is able to share his masculinity with his children, and show them how to attempt to overcome barriers and failures. The father's powerful desire to see his child conquer problems and be self-sufficient causes him to react this way. This is the distinctive role of the father, which the mother, whose paramount concern is her child's physical well-being, cannot fulfill.

In the same way, a father has a special role to play in the moral formation of his children. People talk a lot today about unconditional love, and how important it is. But I think it is a father's role not to heap unconditional love on his children, and simply tell them, "Oh, I love you no matter what you do, no matter how you treat people, and no matter what you become." No, a mother can take that approach. But I think a father's role—indeed, his job— is to place his children under obligation. He must hold them accountable for their behavior. He is to be their primary moral guide and influence. He must let his children know with certainty that how they behave, and the moral habits they thereby cultivate, is an extremely important matter. The father is to be the moral guide and the ethical teacher. A mother, inclined as she is to love her children no matter what they do or what kind of character they develop, is not as able as a father to communicate to kids that there are consequences to how they behave. A father, to be an effective leader to his children, must make it clear to them that how they behave is going to affect how he feels toward them. In this way he communicates to them the gravity of their conduct, the significance of the manner in which they treat other people.

The father imperative is so strong, that even mainstream culture—which has been profoundly feminized—is finally starting to recognize the centrality of fatherhood. Sociologist Barbara Whitehead has succinctly explained why:

> Children in single-parent families are six times as likely to be poor. They are also likely to stay poor longer...[They] are two to three times as likely as children in two-parent families to have emotional and behavioral problems. They are also more likely to drop out of high school, to get pregnant as teenagers, to abuse drugs, and to be in trouble with the law. Compared with children in intact families, children from disrupted families are at a much higher risk for physical or sexual abuse.[3]

If that is not enough to convince, more recently, a definitive study found what commonsense has been telling people for years: fatherless boys tend to become violent and irresponsible men. Among the study's findings were:

• Boys raised outside of marriages are more than twice as likely as other boys to end up in jail.

• Each year a boy spends without a dad in the home raises the odds of his future incarceration by about five percent.

• A boy needs to spend time with his dad. A child born to an unwed mother is roughly two and one half times as likely to be imprisoned, while a boy whose parents split while he is a teenager is only one and a half times as likely to be imprisoned.

• Among the study's other findings that explode liberal myths: a boy living with his single father, as opposed to his single mother, faced no more higher risk of incarceration than do children from intact homes, so obviously, fathers are indispensable; child support payments from a father, that is, mere dollars without the father's presence, made no difference in the likelihood a boy will grow up to become a criminal; and, while poor kids are more likely to be incarcerated as adults, family structure was the most important aspect of their lives in determining their future.[4]

Sociologist Maggie Gallagher nicely summarizes the conclusions of this study:

> [T]he attachment between father and son may be the key [to responsible boys]. Fathers teach their sons lessons, directly and indirectly, about what it means to be a man. When boys identify with fathers who are loving and available, the likelihood lessens that they will define their masculinity in terms of rebellion and antisocial aggression.[5]

Until we begin to emphasize the necessity of fathers—to girls as well as boys—we are not going to stop producing unhappy kids, who cannot get along with the opposite sex. The male-female relationship problems of today have their roots in the family dysfunctions and fragmentations of 10, 20 and 30 years ago.

The only way to break this cycle is to assert the centrality of fatherhood to society, and understand that men and women have enduring, God-ordained differences that are not merely, as the feminists say, "socially conditioned." Indeed, it is far more likely that the feminists themselves have been socially conditioned to attribute all gender differences to social conditioning, rather than to nature. Their movement is nothing less than a tyranny, and one dead-set against the traditional family. As Robert H. Bork has noted, "Feminism is not about giving women freedom to choose; it is about taking away choices of which feminists disapprove. And one choice they disapprove is participation in a conventional family."[6]

Yet it is the traditional family, with the father as leader and head, that will be the salvation of our civilization. This concept is deeply hated by liberals and misandrist feminists. It is, nonetheless, utterly true, and our society is finding it out the hard way. Indeed, proof of this is the national discussion now taking place of what has come to be known as the "boyfriend problem." Children need their fathers living with them, not just any man, such as the single mother's boyfriend. One recent study found that live-in boyfriends are 27 times more likely to abuse a child than that child's natural father.[7] I have, for years, been saying that this "boyfriend problem" is epidemic in the black community, and, of course, I get attacked when I do so. Time after time I have counseled with young black women in their late teens or early twenties, who now have deep psychological problems stemming from the sexual abuse they suffered at the hands of their mother's live-in boyfriends. One such woman I recently saw, Pat, 20 years old, was in drug rehab and trying to earn the high school diploma she never got, because she had to leave school, flee her house, and stay on the streets to get away from her mother's "boyfriend," who molested her and beat her mother.

But finally someone else is speaking out about this horror in black families. Anne Thompson-Scretching, a black female playwright who wrote a play about this subject entitled "You Shouldn't Have Told," says "For a long time, this was a taboo subject, especially in the black community."[8] Her play has brought these issues to light, and as more and more black people speak out, even if they are called "Uncle Toms" or "Sellouts" for doing so, our communities can begin to heal.

Of course, this problem is culture-wide, and it is perpetuated by the intellectually lazy habit of liberalism to avoid being "judgmental," especially of females' and minorities' behavior. As David Blankenhorn notes, "To bring up the boyfriend problem seems too much like you're passing judgment on the sexual behavior of single mothers."[9] And under the regime of politically-correct feminism, that is forbidden, no matter how many children suffer.

If we as a culture began to embrace the centrality of fatherhood to both the psychological and emotional well-being of children and the stability of our society, we would begin to see massive improvements in our children and the qualities of the families they form as adults.

Black Men, Black Women

The ideas of white female feminists have been especially destructive in the black community. By advocating role reversal and a general female anger across America, these privileged white women have harmed black families by hindering their unity and healing. Any family, as an organic entity, has a natural healing inclination. It wants to heal itself, and function well for the sake of all involved, especially the children. But the ideology of white feminists, which is nothing less than rage at men and America generally, is not relevant to black women, whose major problems have always been of a more practical and less theoretical nature.

The black woman wants her man to be there for her and her children, to work hard, to control himself sexually, and to provide for his family. She is not concerned about the "oppressive patriarchy" that privileged white women prattle on and on about. White feminists, who wish to change the basic structure of American society (and to a significant extent have already succeeded at doing so), have an interest in maintaining social chaos and change. The momentum today of homosexuality, abortion on demand, silly sexual harassment suits and so on is all to their liking, because it fits their agenda of social revolution. These white women are angry at their fathers, and they are angry at men generally. So these feminists, seeking to trash the nation at which they are so angry, support hostility between the black man and the black woman, because they are trying to enlist the black woman in their cause of complete social change. The black woman is used—through welfare programs, through affirmative action programs, through abortion—to promote the agenda of elite liberal white women. And black civil rights leaders are perfectly happy to let this happen, because they are in league with white feminists to advance their own power. The members of the liberal coalition of race and gender grievance groups tend first to their own needs, not those of their putative constituencies.

The truth is though, that black men and black women are perfectly capable of solving their problems on their own, without the meddling of the feminist establishment. But unfortunately, feminists' seeds of discord have already been sown, mainly through their ethic of role reversal.

Indeed, a primary reason black men and women don't get along today is the role-reversal between them. During the last 40 years or so, the black woman has largely assumed the role of the man. She has become the primary provider and authority figure for the home. This causes resentment on the part of black women. They are dissatisfied with their men for not fulfilling their rightful role of provider and caretaker for their families. Black women have, then, become hostile toward their men who they see as insecure and weak, as men who, in short, remind them of their fathers, who often demonstrated these same qualities.

When a woman has to take on both the role of mother and father, as so often happens in black America where so many men have dropped out of society, she becomes, quite naturally, hostile. Her daughters live with this hostility, and, as adults, manifest it towards men, and have trouble getting along with them. This, combined with frequent male irresponsibility, especially sexually, continues the cycle of anger in the black family that prevents black men and women from getting along well. Female hostility in the black family gets passed on from generation to generation, and black men don't know how to deal with this anger and are somewhat intimidated by it, because it was the same anger that was in their mothers. This unsettling cycle prevents the black man from taking his role of leadership in the black family.

The history of slavery and Jim Crow has something to do with this disabling of the black family, but it doesn't fully explain it, because under much of racial oppression, the black family remained very strong, and largely intact. During slavery, women understood that if their husbands were taken away, it was by force. Their anger was not directed primarily at their husbands, therefore. But today, male abandonment is really a choice. Whether through literal physical abandonment, or figuratively, through ineffectiveness, the man leaves his family. Either way, female anger is fomented, and family recovery is made more difficult.

Black women have seen white women take on the responsibilities of men even when they didn't have to, and this has only validated, in the minds of black women, the role of provider many of them took on out of necessity. This of course then demotivated black women from seeking to place their black men back as heads of their houses, because they now found themselves a part of a larger cultural trend. For the black man, recovering leadership in his family has been made more difficult by white feminists and their social renovations.

The Black Man at Home

Black men, abused throughout so much of history, wish to responsibly rule their families. They want to fulfill their role as men, and as husbands. As with all people, they have a deep sense of what they should be doing, even if they are failing at it. In counseling, I have met many men on drugs, chasing women, and drinking constantly, who are miserable living that way. They know they are failing their families, and failing as men. They know they should re-embrace responsibility.

I have found that men, even dysfunctional men, are motivated by the call to headship. They know that the man should be the head of the family, and he should act like it. Now, let me stress that male-headship doesn't mean that the man is better than the woman, or that he should be served by her. Its significance lies in organization. Given the internal constitution of men and women, the family simply works better that way. It is its organic structure. Many women today, infected by feminism, will say that this type of order is unfair. But in my experience, women actually prefer their man to be the head of their family. Women want a strong, reliable, good-hearted man to lead them. They want to be able to depend on their man, to trust him, and to know that he will provide for them in every way, and be faithful to them. Yet, even though women really want this, few will publicly say so, because if they do, they are likely to be laughed at, or criticized, by other women who are envious of them and are personally unhappy in their own lives.

The black man especially, having been belittled and humiliated historically, yearns to fulfill his role as the leader of his family. He desperately wants to demonstrate his competence as a man. Tragically, the confusions of our day about male and female nature, and the roles of men and women, do not provide a social context which makes it easy for him to accomplish that. This leads to a frustration on his part, which, coupled with the pre-existent hostility of the black woman, makes many black families angry places. This is a tragedy. If black families overcame their anger, blacks in America would make more progress than a thousand NAACP initiatives would yield. In fact, if these advocacy groups really want to help black people, they should focus on families not politics, because that is where the most important problems facing blacks are to be found. As Dennis Prager is fond of saying, "What happens in your house is more important than what happens in the White House."

True Masculinity

We are confused today about men and women, and their proper roles and ways of relating, because, quite frankly, as a society we have largely abandoned belief in the Judeo-Christian God. People today give lip service to religion, but they often don't really mean it. We talk the talk, but we don't walk the walk. Yet, if we returned to the simple faith of our forefathers, and genuinely made pleasing God the most important quest of our lives, this country's moral decline would reverse, and the way men and women relate to one another would improve. Gender confusion is really the product of moral relativism. We don't know who we are anymore, or what our respective roles are, because we have declared individual behavior a matter of taste, not objective morality.[10] Moral relativism has led men, especially in fragmented black families, to abandon their families, to be sexually promiscuous, to avoid work, and to rely on women. And women, in response, often act like men, particularly in the black community. When a people abandons the practice of a common ethics rooted in a personally and socially transcendent God, they invite the twin disasters of male irresponsibility and female aggression. We find these realities commonly in black families.

But when God is first in a man's life, he becomes responsible, and the shine of true manhood is upon him. Women respect men who love God and demonstrate responsibility, and they willingly submit to such men. When this takes place, order is restored in the family, in intimate relationships, and in people's lives as a whole.

The truly masculine man is one who loves what is right. The masculine man loves truth more than anything else. He is not ego-driven, he is driven by what is right. He is not ruled by his desire for sex, but he is ruled by his desire to honor God. He looks to God to guide him, and to the true knowledge he has about himself. He does not rely on women for approval and satisfaction. Many men today, confused about their own masculinity, look to women to guide them, because they figure that way they can avoid being criticized by women, and then they will feel secure as men. These men are looking to women for emotional support. But a real man never looks to women for emotional support, because as a true man he is not driven by emotions, he is not dependent on them whatsoever. His behavior is not motivated by the need for other people's approval, he is motivated by the truth alone, and he has the strength of character to go ahead and do what is right, no matter how much he is criticized by his confused peers.

The true man is self-reliant and self-confident. His family naturally looks up to him, and others find it easy to respect him. People have high regard for him because they sense he is competent, that he knows what is right and is committed to it, and is not driven by what he feels or what others expect of him. He is a man of decent character, who always treats others fairly, and un-failingly looks after the interests of his family. This is authentic masculinity, and it is best found and formed in the context of traditional religious faith.

The Place of Sex

But this is certainly not the view of masculinity that prevails to-day. In our morally bewildered country, the lifestyle of Larry Flynt or Hugh Hefner is what passes for masculinity. There tends to be a stupid equation of number of sex partners with level of mas-culinity. But simply having sex is not a measure of a man at all. Anyone can have an erection, that doesn't take any strength of character or self-discipline.

But our sexually obsessed culture teaches men that if they are really a man, they will be sexually loose. Ironically, women's maga-zines are major proponents of this idea, urging women to relate to men on a sexual level first. Read the covers of *Ebony, Cosmo-politan, Allure,* or *Marie Claire;* they are all about sex, and how to please a man sexually. These magazines are catering to a market in rebellion against the man-hating anger of 1970s and 1980s feminism. Yet these are sexually manipulative and confused women, who understand neither the nature of sex nor love. They would do well to reflect on the old saying that I think is abso-lutely true, and accurately states the different inclinations of both men and women: *women give sex to get love, men give love to get sex.*

The basic problem with sex and sexuality today is that it is identified as "love," and with feelings of deep intimacy and mean-ing. But of course, just because two people have had sex, that doesn't mean they're in love. Young people today confuse the two, and so believe that they are fulfilling their true purpose as men and women, by simply being sexual together. But their true purpose is to form and guide a stable family together. Mistaking sex for love causes people to misunderstand their real mission as a man or a woman, and so they neglect strong character and family formation for the sake of sexual activity. This psychological mistake has hindered men and women from successfully relating to each other, and as a later consequence, it also thwarts the formation of sound families. We need to think properly about sex, and recognize its limited place, valuing responsibility more than pleasure. The fact some people think that nearly impossible, is only a testament to how far we have fallen culturally.

There was, recently, a stunning case in point of the kind of thinking that is destroying our nation today, and causing people to experience so much pain in their lives because of sexual mistakes. In a classic example of the madness of today's liberalism, actress Sharon Stone assured the United Nations, "No matter how much we guide our children within our families, within our churches, within our schools, we are not stronger than the power of sexuality—particularly to a teen-ager." She went on, "I believe that if you truly, truly love your children, you need to supply condoms in a place in your home…. I mean, put 200 condoms in a box in some place in the house where everybody isn't all the time so that your kids can take them."[11] This, from a childless, multi-millionaire Hollywood elitist. I want to say this as simply and as clearly as possible: Ms. Stone is absolutely, without a shred of doubt, 100% wrong. Her advice would ruin millions of families. Yet tragically, her views are largely the norm today, which is why she was asked to address the United Nations.

The Path to Recovery

Well, what is the path to recovery? How can men and women get along better, and live at peace with themselves and each other?

To begin with, they need to realize that their warfare—inside of themselves and with each other—is spiritual first. It is nothing less than a warfare between good and evil, between order and disorder, stability and chaos. The sooner they realize that, the sooner they can start to heal.

Second, people have to realize that their most important battles are within themselves, not in the external culture. Men and women should know that self-control is essential both to individual happiness, and to happiness with the other sex. No man can be happy with a woman, and no woman can be content with a man, unless first each person is able to control their anger, emotions, and sex drive. To do that, people need to know where their anger came from and how it got started, so they can effectively deal with those personal issues, and then move on into the future. Just as I had to forgive my parents for their failures and lack of love for me, so people today need to search their hearts, discover the origins of their anxiety and discontent, and forgive those who have wronged them. Then they can operate in their proper state of being, and function efficiently and with stability. Coming to this place of maturity will help men and women both to stop using sex as a surrogate for real intimacy and love and to stop using sex as a kind of opiate to ease the pain of a dysfunctional personal life. With this understanding, women will no longer employ sex as a means of manipulating men, and men will not see sex as a merely recreational activity, with no attendant obligations.

Thus, we will stop using each other, and humanize our relationships with the opposite sex. We can then grow as people. We will love one another with truth and not with mere emotion, with a genuine depth of feeling and not the false feelings of affection that unprincipled sexual activity can give.

Chapter Four

THE PROBLEM WITH ABORTION

How dare you tell women abortion is wrong! For many women,
especially black women, abortion means personal freedom!
 —*A black woman who manages an inner-city abortion clinic,*
   confronting Jesse during his protest of her business.

It is one of the great ironies of our time that those who pass for
"black leaders" are so vocal about every perceived racial slight,
and yet are not only silent—but even supportive—of the most
overt and destructive attack on black Americans: abortion on
demand.

Abortion is unique among political issues. While debates about
affirmative action, gerrymandering, and tax policy are important,
they are not life and death issues. Abortion is. It is an undeniable
fact that every abortion kills a human being.[1] And it is an undeniable fact that the practice of abortion in this country is immensely harmful, first to the pre-born human being it kills, but
then also in less obvious ways to the woman who aborts, to the
man who participates in abortion, and to the larger culture.

Since abortion—even though it is the primary skirmish of the
contemporary culture war—is still a topic shrouded in mystery
and misinformation, I will first bring before us the true nature
and meaning of abortion, then focus on its significance for black
America (a subject profoundly underdiscussed). I will conclude
this chapter by examining what abortion practice does to human
relationships, including how it affects the most important purpose in a man's life: fatherhood.

Abortion: The Ultimate Betrayal

"Choice" is the word of the day. Everything from watches to cars to insurance is sold by appeal to your "right to choose." This is how profoundly deep our cultural absorption of the rhetoric of abortion rights has been. "Choice" is a clever word for the abortion establishment to fly as its banner, since it reminds us of freedom and liberty. It has positive emotional connotations. But when we look carefully at the use of the word "choice" in the context of abortion, we can see how utterly meaningless it really is.

Choice itself is bankrupt as an ethical concept. Many people today believe that merely because they have made a behavioral choice or selected a position on a given topic or issue, their decision is therefore morally right and immune from critical evaluation. But the act of making a choice does not by itself make that choice right or good. "Choice" is not itself a moral value. It is only a faculty of the will. It is neither good nor bad in itself. Choice—the act of making a decision—alone, without any social context, is just a mechanical mental operation, like adding two and two.

But does the mere fact that a decision has been made automatically render that decision morally right? Of course not. The worth of our decisions and expressions of freedom depends on the courses decided or the ends chosen. The moral quality of our choices is wholly determined by what it is we have chosen to do and why we have chosen it. The absolutizing of freedom in contemporary American life and the automatic rightness accorded actions done by individual "choice" obscures this, and protects the work of "choice" and "self-expression" from moral criticisms of even the simplest sort.

The truth is in other areas of life; free from the confusing fog of political correctness enshrouding consideration of pre-natal human life and abortion, we routinely—as individuals and as a public—approve or disapprove of individual and social choices based on the content of those choices. We need to evaluate morally the substance of our choices. Right and wrong are independent of our emotions, they are not decided by them. The abortion ethic denies this commonsense idea.

The consequences of this country's basic declaration that we can't make a moral judgment about abortion are horrific. Foremost among them, is the near complete dehumanization of the fetus. No longer deemed part of the human community, pre-natal human beings are commonly disparaged and victimized. Consider this gruesome resume of inhumanity:

• George Tiller, a Wichita, Kansas abortionist who specializes in late term abortions, has said, "the woman is the patient and the fetus is the problem...this is as big as a cancer, as big as a malignancy."[2] In Dr. Tiller's place of business it is routine for him to commit ten to twenty late second- and third-trimester abortions each week, in which several women at a time lie on cots in a room in his clinic basement, laboring to deliver their nearly full-term—but dead—babies. Tiller advertises widely, including on the internet, and charges from $1,850 to $3,000, cash only, for each abortion, incinerating the aborted babies in his own basement crematorium on the premises.[3]

• Said the father of Melissa Drexler, when asked if he could forgive his daughter—the high school senior who gave birth in the bathroom during her prom, then killed her baby and left him in the bathroom trashcan before returning to the dance floor—"There's nothing to forgive."[4]

• Brian Peterson and Amy Grossberg, the wealthy New Jersey teens who gave birth to their baby in a Delaware motel room then promptly threw the child into a dumpster where he died, were sentenced to 24 and 30 months in jail respectively, and ordered to perform community service as well, which, perversely, the wise judge in their case said should include "counseling teenagers on parenthood." Meanwhile, a Wisconsin man is given 12 years in prison for killing several cats.[5]

• A woman in Wisconsin was charged with attempted homicide for purposely trying to drink her nearly full-term baby to death. The woman's defense attorney argued that the woman had not committed a crime by law, because her alcoholic assault on her pre-born child took place before the baby had been born.

Absurdly, the attorney asserted, "The alleged victim was not a human being." The baby, named Meagan, had been born after the woman's drinking binge, with facial abnormalities, including a compressed nose and wide-set eyes. Her future mental abilities are not known. The baby was placed in foster care, where her progress has been reported as slow.[6]

• Recently a woman shot herself in the stomach in order to kill the 20-week fetus inside of her. The baby survived the attack, was born alive, but later died after efforts to save him. The woman, 19 years of age, was charged with third-degree murder and manslaughter.[7] Of course, had she aborted in an abortion clinic, killing the child at the same stage of development and even later, it would have been perfectly legal.

• In 1993 a 24-week-old fetus received life-saving surgery while still *in-utero*.[8] But had the mother wished to have this fetus killed through abortion, in every state of the nation it would have been legal for her to do so. In a similar case, Noah Kipfmiller, born in early 1998, received life-saving surgery while he was still in the womb. He was suffering with spina bifida, a serious congenital defect which often results in the mother having an abortion. But this miraculous surgery, performed on Noah when his mother was 23 weeks pregnant with him, saved his life. His mother could have walked into any abortion clinic in this country and paid a doctor to kill Noah, at the same age he had life-saving surgery.[9]

• A man in Texas was convicted of manslaughter when, while driving drunk, he hit a car in which a seven-and-a-half month pregnant woman was riding. The baby girl was born shortly after the accident, and within two days died from injuries she suffered as a result of the accident. In language that was Orwellian and yet chillingly honest, the last sentence of the article about this tragedy reads, "Abortion rights supporters warned that it [the conviction of the drunk driver] could lead to a new determination of when life begins, and, eventually, the outlawing of abortion."[10]

• In California, the state Supreme Court has held that someone who causes the death of a fetus as early as seven weeks can be charged with fetal murder.[11] This does not apply to doctors who, with the mothers' consent, cause the death of fetuses sometimes much later in pregnancy.

• The ACLU argued that a 1970 California law against fetal murder could not be used against a pregnant woman who caused the stillbirth of her full-term baby by going on a two-day drug spree just before the child's birth, because the law violated the woman's right to privacy by intruding on her freedom to make decisions about childbearing and health care.[12] In California such prenatal abuses of the fetus are usually not prosecuted, in deference to strongly influential feminist lobbies and the powerful abortion establishment.[13]

Indeed, our culture's dehumanization of the pre-born is so complete, and our elites' commitment to abortion so emphatic, that tortured readings of laws are given in order to protect the status quo of abortion practice. Thus, a California appeals court ruled that a law punishing one parent for beating another doesn't apply to pregnant women. The court argued pregnant women aren't really mothers, since the word "mother" is defined in the law in a way that makes "the birth of a child...an essential prerequisite."[14] So all you pregnant ladies, that morning sickness you're having, that kicking you feel in your stomach, and those ultrasound pictures you have on your refrigerator—you're just hallucinating, you're not really a mother.

There is no question that every abortion kills a human being before his birth. Deep down, everyone really knows this. The unborn human being has a unique and permanent genetic identity (since conception); a beating heart (since three-and-a-half weeks); detectable brain activity (since six weeks); fully formed fingers, toes, and all internal organs (since eight weeks).[15] By three months this human being is forming fists, bending arms, curling toes, and rapidly growing. This is not a potential life; it is an actual life, with potential. This reality is so compelling that even leading pro-choice feminists like Naomi Wolf have acknowledged it, and called for their comrades to frankly admit that every abortion kills a human life.

Nevertheless, professional advocates of legal abortion persist in feigning wonderment at whether or not the fetus is a living human being. The logic against them could not be more elementary. First, the unborn entity is an actual being, it is alive. If this were not so, there would be no need for an abortion. The very purpose of the abortion is to kill that which is alive. Second, this being is human. What else could it be? Feline? Canine? Bovine? As Congressman Henry Hyde once quipped, "No woman has ever given birth to a Golden Retriever." Human beings give birth to human beings. It is disingenuous to claim that a fetus is not a definite, living human being. Those who have seen ultrasound images of pre-born babies have eyewitness, empirical evidence of the unborns' living humanity.

In an insightful yet simple attempt to make plain the logically and biologically necessary conclusion that every human life begins at conception, psychologist Sidney Callahan writes, "If we took a movie of everyone alive and ran it backward, we would see that we are continuous with our embryonic beginnings...we can rationally infer that the child and the infant—and before that the fetus and the embryo—are continuously us."[16]

This truth was tellingly borne out by the experience of one Los Angeles obstetrician, who wrote of why he no longer does abortions. After the onset of depression and self-hate following years of abortion practice, Dr. George Flesh explained how his change of heart came about:

> Early in my practice, a married couple came to me and requested an abortion. Because the patient's cervix was rigid, I was unable to dilate it to perform the procedure. I asked her to return in a week, when the cervix would be softer.
>
> The couple returned and told me that they had changed their minds and wanted to "keep the baby." I delivered the baby seven months later. Years later, I played with little Jeffrey in the pool at the tennis club where his parents and I were members. He was happy and beautiful. I was horrified to think that only a technical obstacle had prevented me from terminating Jeffrey's potential life.[17]

So Jeffrey's is one life spared from the grisly altar of "choice."
He is one of the lucky ones.

Why then the slaughter of the innocents? The basic answer is
simple: pure selfishness. We are a selfish people, we want to do
what we want, no matter what, and so we allow this most selfish
and unnatural act. Of course, opportunistic politicians are only
too eager to cater to this irresponsible and unreflective self-
centeredness. They find it easier to say to people seeking abortion,
"OK, go ahead, do whatever you choose," rather than to remind
people of their moral duty not to harm the innocent. Consider
these five famous politicians who used to be pro-life, but now,
because it is convenient to them, spout the slogans of "choice."

—Bill Clinton once wrote in a letter, "I am opposed to abortion and to government funding of abortions. We should not
spend state funds on abortions because so many people believe
abortion is wrong."

—Richard Gephardt, minority leader of the House of Repre-
sentatives, wrote in 1977: "Life...begins at conception. The [Su-
preme Court's abortion ruling] was unjust, and it is incumbent
on the Congress to correct the injustice." Later, in 1984, he wrote,
"I believe that the life of the unborn should be protected at all
costs."

—In 1984 Al Gore stated in a letter to a constituent his "deep
personal conviction that abortion is wrong," and he voted to
change the Civil Rights Act so that it would define the term
"person" to "include unborn children from the moment of conception." Mr. Gore no longer believes prenatal children deserve
protection.

—Senator Edward Kennedy wrote in 1971 that "human life,
even at its earliest stages, has a certain right which must be recognized—the right to be born, the right to love, the right to grow
old."[18]

—Jesse Jackson used to speak out against the abortion culture,
and on behalf of the unborn. He once asked: "What happens to
the mind of a person, and the moral fabric of a nation that accepts the abortion of the life of a baby without a pang of con-

science? What kind of a person, and what kind of a society, will we have 20 years hence if life can be taken so casually?"[19]

The answer, of course, is a very selfish and brutal one. Accompanying the encoding of abortion-selfishness into law—and protecting it—is an elaborate language of dehumanization and denial. Phrases like "right to choose," "ending a pregnancy" and "reproductive freedom" have hypnotized our nation and dulled our conscience. As Michael Bauman of Hillsdale College frankly comments:

> We hide the fetal holocaust that surrounds us every day just as effectively as the Nazis hid their extermination of the Jews. And we do it the same way. We cannot bring ourselves to utter the "M" word, though we commit the "M" act. That is, we do not murder unborn children, we "abort fetuses".... Some of the more squeamish among us are unable even to say the "A" word. Though by aborting fetuses rather than murdering babies our linguistic sleight of hand has hidden the real nature of our action (murder) and the real identity of our victim (baby), some people require a still heavier dose of verbal opium. We must tell them they are merely "terminating a pregnancy," which eliminates overt reference to any living thing.... If "terminating pregnancies" is still too overt a verbal description because the word *pregnant* tends to evoke unfortunate images of happy women large with child, we can hide the crime behind an even more impersonal wall of words. We can say that the murdering of unborn children is nothing more than the voluntary extraction of the "product of conception," or, as nearly all abortion clinics have it, "removing the POC." What could be more innocent.[20]

An important effect of this sanitized language is that it lends to our remarks about the abortion of the unborn the *appearance of reasonableness*. It allows us to believe that we have seriously and forthrightly engaged the full moral meaning of abortion, that we have acted as responsible and mature moral agents. But in fact all we have done is deceive ourselves. We have take our place in the long procession of people who have participated in a rhetorical dance of obfuscation and self-justification regarding the hu-

man target destroyed by the violence of every abortion committed. This participation only works to strengthen the intellectual
atmosphere which shapes the culture of "choice" and our talk of
abortion.

As a culture we conspicuously avoid really talking frankly about
abortion. As one sociologist put it, "[T]here has been virtually no
reporting at all on the debate over the moral status of the fetus.
What is being aborted, after all?"[21]

In abortion and public policy discussions, to raise the topic of
the beauty and awesome nature of nascent human life, details of
fetal development or personal obligations implicated by the value
of the unborn, is to be mocked as "carrying on a love affair with
the fetus," as former surgeon general Joycelyn Elders once said
abortion opponents did—to their great shame, in her eyes. For
Dr. Elders and those of her ilk—as her remarks imply—the human fetus is not a legitimate object of love. Deep concern for it is
a mistake, and fetal life is not worthy of the sort of close attention and reflection one associates with an affection as intense as
"love." This is an extremely significant understanding rooted in
much of American culture. Of course, the irony of Dr. Elders,
formerly the leading national health officer—*and a pediatrician*—
holding such a view is great. It is a testimony to the depth to
which unborn human life has been denigrated and dehuman-
ized. Thirty years after the advent of institutionalized abortion
practice, the human fetus is not to be regarded as an appropriate
object of love. This disturbing reality is only underlined by the
fact that the perspective Dr. Elders' remarks reflect is one that
dominates among bureaucratic, political and media elites.

All of which helps incline the body politic to the fiction that
"compassion" requires us as a nation to embrace liberal abortion
laws. This is an extremely powerful moral judgment in American
life. It has ascended to the level of "public truth"—that is, a generally accepted, unquestioned feature of the social and cultural
landscape. There is no such thing as being compassionate to the
unborn. Not only are they not accorded the legal status of persons, but they are not even allowed into public discussion as le-

gitimate objects of concern. Thus, the devaluation of their lives is not just a legal and moral reality, it is largely a patterned response of the public consciousness itself.

To realize the power of this settledness, we only need note that opinion polls consistently show that most Americans oppose the morality and legality of most abortions performed and that most Americans are stunningly ignorant of current abortion law.[22] The result: abortions—throughout the three trimesters of pregnancy—continue at the rate of about 1.4 million annually.[23]

But even though the contemporary flavor of American culture and society devalues pre-born human life and inhibits open, comprehensive public reflection on it, there is no question that Americans are becoming less comfortable with the regime of abortion on demand. People are growing more aware of the use of abortion as after-the-fact contraception, and of the rhetoric of choice as an asylum from personal moral responsibility, for both women and men.[24] In fact, most people who say they are "pro-choice" actually tend to disapprove of the legality and morality of many abortions, when particular circumstances are identified.[25] Significantly, the number of people who say they support legal abortion under any circumstances has dropped eight percentage points since 1994.[26]

But overcoming the ethical complacency and conversational controls to which we as a social body have become accustomed is difficult. These habits of our society are able to stunt the reporting of even the most morally perverse and ethically repelling transgressions of the abortion culture. For example:

• A pioneering new method for late second- and third-trimester abortions—the "partial birth abortion" or D & X (Dilation and Extraction)—calls for the doctor to pull all of the baby except the head down into the vagina. The doctor then takes a pair of blunt scissors and forces the scissors into the base of the baby's skull, spreading it to enlarge the opening. Using a suction catheter, he then sucks out the brain of the human being, killing it. Dr. Martin Haskell, who teaches the procedure to other doctors at National Abortion Federation seminars, has done this more than 700 times to unborn babies 20 to 26 weeks developed.[27]

• A Los Angeles doctor who operates two abortion clinics is called "an unselfish and committed provider" by a judge who sentenced him to one year probation for the deaths of two women to whom he was administering abortions.[28] Later, following review by the Medical Board of California, the doctor, who has performed approximately 100,000 abortions, has his medical license revoked.[29]

• The commitment of many liberal groups to the abortion culture is absolute. For example, the ACLU protested the efforts of a coalition of churches to provide a dignified burial for 54 aborted pre-born human beings that an abortion clinic had dumped in a vacant field in southern California. The ACLU threatened to sue the coroner who released the bodies to the churches, claiming the funeral service would be a violation of church and state.[30]

Of course, there are consequences to treading the violent path we have. We cannot flaunt the order of nature and believe we will just get away with it. There are three obvious results of the abortion culture as seen in what it does to children, women, and society.

Consequence: Harm to Children

First and most obviously, the devaluation of prenatal children leads to the devaluation of postnatal children. There has been a 331% increase in cases of child abuse during the last two decades, while abortion became firmly institutionalized.[31] The number of murders of children under one year old has increased by 92% during the last 25 years, that is, since the legalization of abortion on demand.[32] Fully one out of ten fetuses in the United States is exposed to cocaine in the womb, affecting 300,000 babies a year.[33]

And the killing of newborns has become nearly routine. Two teenagers in New Jersey secretly gave birth and threw their infants into trash cans; two in New York did the same; a USC student allegedly sent hers down her apartment building's trash chute; and three other Southern California women tossed their newborn babies into garbage bags. Such stories have by now become routine.

While furrowed-browed psychologists and anguished social workers speak to us of "pregnancy denial" and issue vague calls for "education," an obvious and primary cultural cause for this atrocity remains undiscussed: pro-choice rhetoric has ignored the value of prenatal life by absolutely denying that women have any objective obligations toward the fetuses they carry. The constant and prominent repetition of the mantra, "A woman can do what she wants with her own body," has firmly set within our social consciousness the devaluation—indeed, the denial—of human fetal life which it plainly communicates. Thus, schooled in the moral relativism of their "right to choose," some pregnant young women wishing to evade motherhood choose to cross the increasingly porous boundary into infanticide.

With the abortion rights rhetoric of fetal dehumanization so intense and pervasive, why should it surprise us if immediately after her baby's birth an anxious young woman is unwilling to suddenly invest authentic humanity in this person who just moments before was—according to her society—not a person at all, but only a legally disposable part of her body, akin to a bothersome lock of hair or unsightly mole?

It is a fact that in our information and media saturated country, the air we breathe is thick with ideas which inevitably affect our behavior to some degree. Indeed, it is a primary principle of contemporary liberalism that social environment not only influences, but actually determines individual human conduct. Hence, to the liberal mind: poverty causes crime; patriarchy and sexism wound girls' self esteem causing them to underachieve and unnecessarily limit their own career options; and the American history of slavery and Jim Crow creates a crippling residual racism that causes self-loathing and self-destructive behavior among many black Americans. But now, because pregnancy neglect and infanticide call into question the wisdom of modern liberalism's

cherished abortion license, we are to believe that impressionable
young women's treatment of their pre-born and newborn babies
is somehow completely immune from the impact of the ideas
comprising our public conversation about maternal responsibility and prenatal life.

The connection between the dehumanization of pre-born babies, which has been a staple of American abortion advocacy,
and the literal trashing of unwanted newborns is clear and direct.
But it cannot be openly recognized, because to suggest that the
abortion license is tearing at the fine fabric of civil society is to
wonder if perhaps the opening of the abortion floodgates was a
mistake. To court such ideas is to breach the sensitive lines of
liberal orthodoxy, and to invite the intimidating scorn of the powerful abortion lobby, the feminist establishment, and reporters
who disagree. Most of us would rather spare ourselves the head-
ache, and so we are content simply to remain silent about the
social corrosiveness of abortion on demand, and instead express
shock, shock, that a mother could treat her baby like garbage.

Consequence: Harm to Women

Women are also often harmed by abortion, but the supposed pro-
tectors of women—feminists—are silent about this embarrass-
ing fact. Many women grieve deeply after abortion, and they are
affected for decades after having one, sometimes for the rest of
their lives. Writes one woman, "After [my] abortion I had to receive psychiatric assistance. Did it help? Not really. For over 27
years I have lived with the guilt and sorrow of aborting my child.
I can only wonder if counseling services today are giving women
the options that I was not given, or are they still promoting abortion?"[34]

Nancyjo Mann, founder of Women Exploited By Abortion
had a similar reaction. Of her abortion she wrote, "For two hours
I could feel her struggling inside me. But then, as suddenly as it
began, she stopped. Even today, I remember her very last kick on
my left side. She had no strength left. She gave up and died.
Despite my grief and guilt, I was relieved that her pain was fi-

nally over. But I was never the same again. The abortion killed not only my daughter, it killed a part of me."[35]

Of course, it is also true that many women aren't bothered by abortion, and just don't take abortion seriously at all. For example, one woman unabashedly told a national news magazine that she's had about 9 abortions, she can't remember the exact number anymore. "I just kept getting pregnant," she explained.[36] But women like this are harmed in moral and spiritual ways they don't even understand. Her capacity to love as a human being has been shattered by her habitual abortions. Her sensitivity to the suffering of other people has been dulled, and, in all likelihood, her zest for life has faded. It is a testament to the harm abortion does to women that pro-life groups are disproportionately staffed by women of childbearing age.[37] These women intuitively sense what abortion often does to a woman.

And the harm to women is not only spiritual or psychological. It is sometimes physical as well. Consider the case of Sharon Hamptlon. Bruce Steir, a San Francisco abortion doctor who flew up and down the state of California plying his trade, was charged with the killing of Sharon Hamptlon, a black woman of 27 who died after Steir performed an abortion on her which punctured her uterus and left her in unstable condition, vomiting blood. Prosecutors alleged Dr. Steir hurried away from the Southern California abortion clinic after Miss Hamptlon's procedure, even though he knew he had punctured her uterus and that she was bleeding heavily, in very poor condition. Steir was heard telling an assistant he was late for his flight back to the Bay Area. Miss Hamptlon was put in her mother's car and sent home. She died on the way.

At the time of Hamptlon's death, Steir was on probation with the California state medical board. In fact, though he had been regularly performing abortions in clinics both in Northern and Southern California, Steir had been on probation since 1988, for various allegations of incompetence. These included three cases in which women had to have hysterectomies following botched abortions performed by Steir, and one instance in which surgeons had to remove a fetal skull that tore through a woman's uterus after Steir had given her an abortion, leaving the sharp edges of the severed cranium behind.[38]

And recently in Van Nuys, California, an unlicensed "family planning" clinic was the site of an abortion committed by a "physician" which nearly killed a woman, and definitely killed the 6-month-old pre-born human being inside of her who was the target of the "procedure." The third trimester fetus had been stuffed into a garbage bag, and thrown into a dumpster along with the rest of the trash. The abortionist, whose medical license had been suspended, was arrested, held on $1 million bail, and may be charged with murder, because the third-trimester baby was deemed viable. "We've found a lot of things in this place that are disturbing," said one of the police officers who searched the premises, suggesting that the bodies of other dead pre-born human beings were inside.

Such cases are not rare. A doctor in Phoenix recently had his medical license suspended for attempting to abort a teen-ager's full-term baby, and for permitting a woman on whom he was performing an abortion to bleed to death.[39]

These cases came to public light only because of what happened to the women involved. But how many other abortions are performed by rogue doctors of, at best, questionable competence? How can any reasonable person expect that these doctors will manifest a genuine concern for human welfare *when they're in the very business of killing pre-born human beings?* Make no mistake: the overwhelming majority of abortions take place in high-volume clinics, not in the office of a woman's personal physician, and the doctors who harvest huge incomes from manning these mills are sometimes reckless and ruthless. But who will ever know unless something goes wrong? Indeed, their gruesome abortion-work is professionally unsupervised, governmentally unregulated, and publicly undiscussed. The harm done to women in abortion clinics is one of the most underreported stories in this country.

Consequence: Harm to Society

A bizarre doublemindedness exists in American life: we personally and institutionally cherish unborn human beings—and devote substantial resources to save them—while at the same time we personally and institutionally destroy them, all depending upon the pregnant woman's attitude toward them, an attitude often distorted by pressure from the man in her life to abort.

Yet, obviously nothing changes in the nature of the human fetus. The aborted are intrinsically no different from those who survive the vagaries of choice. If allowed to be born they would be as beautiful and full of promise as the wanted. But as a society we have decided that membership in the human family is not determined by biology, rather by a mother's feelings toward her offspring. We have declared that human life does not have absolute value—some lives are worth more than others. This is a dangerous and slippery slope, for whom will we subjectivize next?

How ironic that we agonize every election year over a host of bureaucratic public policy issues, meanwhile we tolerate the ultimate disenfranchisement of an entire class of human beings. The common resort to "I oppose abortion, but I support a woman's right to choose" does not relieve us of this hypocrisy, since no one who holds this confession would allow the killing of people living outside a woman's womb. The logic of choice must perversely hold that the unborn—unless their mother wants them—are not human beings worth including in the human community. Thus, we have accepted the fundamental basis of all human rights violations in the world: the idea that humanity is subjective, and the powerful may bestow human standing on the vulnerable as they will.

The profound contradiction between how we treat the unborn when they are wanted and what we do to them when they are not wanted creates a corrosive social consciousness of "might makes right" and moral relativism. The shallow mental habits cultivated by "choice" convince us that our will to power is morally unproblematic, and our choices self-validating. Yet, some 33 years after the advent of abortion on demand, can we honestly

say that our national soul and moral culture have not been coarsened and brutalized by the selfish anthem, "My body, my choice"?

It is an undeniable objective reality that the unborn are us, just
as we all were once them. Babies are not delivered by the stork: a
birth is the culmination of a natural, continuous and ordered process of growth that began at the union of sperm and egg. Indeed,
the very word "fetus"—Latin for "offspring"—denotes a definite
and fully established type of being at a certain stage of its existence, not a being which is different in kind from what it will later
become. If we better harmonize our social lives with our moral
sense by recognizing the inviolable dignity of each human life,
we will humanize our culture, and move toward living the full meaning of our national creed: all people are created—not born—equal.

The most fundamental harm abortion does to a culture is that
it undercuts love. In an abortion culture, people's ability to love
others decreases, because they come to regard people instrumen-
tally, as objects to be respected only at one's discretion. As
Frederica Mathewes-Green has insightfully written,

> In no sane country are women and their own children assumed
> to be mortal enemies; any culture that so assumes is slowly com-
> mitting suicide. This is true both literally and symbolically as
> well. When we accept as normal the nipping of a child from the
> mother's womb, we violate something disturbingly close to the
> heart of the human story. In the land where women kill their
> unborn children, every lesser love grows frail.[40]

Further, abortion in general insinuates irresponsibility within
a society. The devaluation of children never stays confined to just
the pre-born, but the young, the elderly, and the infirm also come
to be regarded as disposable.

Unfortunately, it is black America and other minority communities who are most affected by the general cultural tendency
toward irresponsibility. Regularly the papers are filled with stories
of abuse and mistreatment of black children by their mothers
and fathers.

Indeed, the irresponsibility of some parents in the black community is mind-boggling, and so is the stupidity of some of the people in the legal system who deal with them. Consider the recent case of Latrena Denise Pixley, a black woman. One day she became annoyed with her crying six-week-old child, so she suffocated her and threw in her in the trash. Pixley spent the rest of the day cooking, and later went out for some barbecue with her boyfriend. Although Pixley pleaded guilty to second-degree murder, Judge George W. Mitchell of Washington, D. C., inexplicably sentenced her only to a short stay in a halfway house. The father of this child was so distraught at this sentence that he killed himself.

After release from the halfway house Pixley gave birth to another out-of-wedlock child. Fortunately, Pixley was quickly returned to prison for credit card fraud and various parole violations, so her new child, Cornelius, had a chance at a healthy childhood in foster-care. But subsequently another judge, Michael Mason, removed Cornelius from foster care and returned him to the newly re-released Latrena Pixley, even though Cornelius' foster mother pleaded with the judge to allow her to adopt Cornelius. The judge said "family preservation" and racial uniformity were important enough to return the boy to Pixley, even though she had murdered his sister. The foster mother was not black, you see, and so Cornelius, who was black, was returned to the similarly colored Pixley. Skin-color, apparently, is more important to some judges than goodness and responsibility. This saga is typical of the destructiveness of the liberal obsession with race, and modern liberalism's failure to emphasize responsibility over rights.[41] It also shows us what can happen in inner-city environs when taking care of the most helpless of children becomes optional to society at large.

What Abortion Really Means for Black America

Of all the populations in the United States, black people should be the ones most outspoken against the slaughter of the innocents. Blacks are the only group—besides the pre-born—who have ever been completely and systematically disenfranchised. Black conservative Peter Kirsanow has noted the striking parallels between the way blacks were treated under slavery, and the way the pre-born are today. He writes,

> The primary tactic in the systematic abuse of any class of people is to dehumanize them. Thus, it cannot be admitted that the unborn child is a person, and it cannot be granted that the unborn child has inalienable rights, including the right to life. A concession that the unborn child is a person would destroy the psychology of denial that makes the decision to abort easier. The identical constructs were used to support slavery. Every attempt was made to deny that blacks were fully human. They didn't look like "us," so they must not be "us." Their humanity could not be allowed to become a public reality. Masters in some colonies were even prohibited from freeing slaves, since to do so might suggest a moral problem with slavery, and somehow communicate the humanity of the enslaved.[42]

But, in fact, because of so many black peoples' unthinking allegiance to the Democratic Party (which is absolutist on abortion and does not permit serious expressions of pro-life sentiment), black people fail to recognize the clear similarity between their history and the plight of the pre-born today, and are some of the most ardent supporters of abortion on demand. For example, Faye Wattleton, Joycelyn Elders, Cynthia Tucker, and of course U. S. Congresswoman Maxine Waters are four nationally prominent black women who have been outspoken supporters of women destroying their offspring.

The great irony, rarely recognized, is that abortion in America was initially conceived and advocated for the purpose of reducing the black population. Margaret Sanger, founder of Planned Parenthood and one of the champions of the abortion rights movement, was an unapologetic eugenicist and a racist, and wanted minorities and the poor to have abortions. Abortion was seen by her as a way of "improving" the population. She did not intend its widespread use among whites, and is famous for her slogan "More [children] from the fit, and less from the unfit." Who are the unfit? The black poor.

In Sanger's view, "Negroes and southern Europeans," as she put it, were simply "mentally inferior to native born Americans," and minorities in general—including Jewish people—were "feeble minded," "human weeds," and "a menace to society."[43] "Blacks...are a menace to the race," she once wrote.[44] To Sanger, the poor were simply irresponsible and stupid.[45] Therefore, she thought, efforts by society should be made to insure that, by means of birth control and abortion, the poor have fewer children.

The undiscussed truth is that Planned Parenthood still operates in line with these ideas today. Planned Parenthood clinics— and abortion clinics generally—are frequently located in inner city areas where they can prey on poor minority women, and receive public funds for doing so.

The effect? A remarkably disproportionate number of black babies are aborted. The abortion rate per 1000 women for whites is 18, for blacks 54, and for others 38.[46] Black women are three times more likely than white women to have an abortion.[47] Those in the business of abortion know this, and so continue to feed lies to blacks about the necessity of legal abortion for their economic well-being. The fact is that there are many people—on both the Left and the Right—who are pro-choice out of a racist motivation to keep the number of blacks in the population as low as possible.[48] That has always been the story of abortion in America.

And yet, thankfully, some of the fiercest opponents of abortion are black, such as Alan Keyes, who once stirringly said,

[How] can [we] look our daughters in the eye and tell them that it is somehow consistent with freedom for them to trample on the human rights of their unborn offspring. We're going to have to find the courage one of these days to tell people that freedom is not an easy discipline. Freedom is not a choice for those who are lazy in their heart and in their respect for their own moral capacities. Freedom requires that at the end of the day you accept the constraint that is required...a respect for the laws of nature and nature's God that say unequivocally that your daughters do not have the right to do what is wrong, that [your] sons do not have the right to do what is wrong. They do not have the right to steal bread from the mouths of the innocent, they do not have the right to steal life from the womb of the unborn.[49]

More black people should be thinking like Alan Keyes, and standing up against the abortion culture which is, in fact, the moral twin of slavery.

The Abortion of Relationships

Another undiscussed reality of abortion practice is the destruction it brings to natural human relationships. Abortion pulls people apart from one another, makes enemies out of friends, and creates deep wounds of anger and bitterness. The abortion establishment is silent on this subject, but abortion brings great pain to human relationships.

Whenever a woman aborts, it brings on guilt in her. No matter how many rationalizations she has heard, and no matter what she tells herself, she knows intuitively that abortion is a great moral evil. This guilt causes her to become angry at the man who impregnated her; this is especially so if he pressures her into having an abortion, which men often do.

Why do men pressure women into aborting? There are two main reasons. First, since abortion is legal and completely acceptable to society, some men feel entitled to compel their girlfriends to abort. Since they don't want to be fathers, or be financially responsible for a child, the lure of abortion is powerful. To their minds, it literally can solve all of their problems. One such man, a medical student, was recently charged with assault and the unauthorized practice of medicine after forcibly restraining his pregnant girlfriend, and repeatedly injecting her with a drug that caused her to miscarry.[50]

Second, men support abortion and encourage women to participate in them because it frees men from sexual responsibility.

As George Weigel explains,

> [*Roe v. Wade*] is alleged to have empowered women; in fact, *Roe* legally disempowered women from holding men accountable for their sexual behavior where that behavior had unplanned results. *Roe's* cultural message has been even more potent than its legal impact, for it effectively eliminated any real world consequences for men who use women as mere instruments of male sexual gratification...*Roe* not only changed our law; it changed the moral culture of America. And it did so to the great disadvantage of women.[51]

Women's advocate Frederica Mathewes-Green echoes this view:

> Abortion [has] not helped women, but it has helped those who would be inconvenienced by her pregnancy and her child. It is easier for a sexually irresponsible man to pay for a woman's abortion than to marry her, or to pay child support for 18 years. It is not out of concern for women's welfare and dignity that *Playboy* so enthusiastically supports abortion on demand.[52]

If black men, and all men, were strong—meaning they love the truth more than they love themselves—they would take responsibility for their sexual actions, and the abortion rate would decline. True masculinity avoids abortion and provides for children, instead of eliminating them.

So the anger women feel, often generated by being coerced by men into abortion, becomes a corrosive force in their lives, poisoning their outlook on life and their relationships with other people. They may even start to mistreat other people, because they are angry and frustrated with themselves.

Of course, on the other hand, abortion sometimes is engaged in *because* of anger. Women know that they can always hurt a man (if he is a real man and loves his children), by paying a doctor to kill his offspring. This is a common occurrence, and, obviously, demolishes what may remain of any friendship between a man and woman. For example, one woman said she had an abortion because without it, "I'd be looking at that dumb man's face in that child and resenting it."[53]

But beyond the anger and hostility that can cause abortion or come from it, abortion also ends relationships between couples who engage in it. After abortion, the attitudes of men and women change toward one another. Trust is gone, affection is diminished, respect is lessened, and playfulness stifled. Many, many couples, married and not, break up after abortion. I remember one young girl I counseled. She was 19, and had recently had an abortion. She said that her boyfriend seemed sullen and angry toward her now, that they didn't talk as much, that the intimacy between them was gone, and he seemed cold and distant. That's what abortion often does: it changes the way people feel toward each other.

But if abortion is so destructive, why is it flourishing in our culture? Whose interests are served by American culture's willful ignorance concerning abortion? Obviously not the unborn child's. Nor can it truly be the woman's, since she must live with the haunting and hurting knowledge of what she has done and what might have been, of a future that might have turned out much brighter than the dark scenarios she imagined, and perhaps believed, possibly as a means of self-justification and emotional self-protection.[54] Rather, the extremely lucrative abortion industry is the entity truly served by this country's general moral complacency about abortion. About half-a-billion dollars a year are generated by the abortion industry, and the organizations that benefit from this money are fierce defenders of abortion. They will cloak their language in pious talk of "women's rights" and "reproductive freedom," but the fact is money is on the line in the continued practice of abortion, and that is the primary motivation of a great many abortion defenders.

Abortion and Fatherhood

Despite long-term liberal denial, the fatherlessness crisis is obvious to all.[55] This is apparent by the simple fact we have already stressed in chapter three, that each night about 40% of American children go to sleep in a home where their fathers do not live.[56] Whether deadbeat dads, absent dads, or men who have never accepted paternity for their children, many American men have decided that their acts of sexual intercourse do not in any way obligate them morally to the offspring that may result. It is an obvious but politically- incorrect possibility that the withering of American fatherhood is significantly related to the liberal social ethos erected the past three decades to support the culture of "choice." If we consider the psychological effects on men of our cultural saturation with the principle of "choice," it's not hard to understand why men are becoming "pro-choice" about fatherhood.

The ethical imperative of "my body, my choice" has meant that women can decide whether or not to give birth once they become pregnant. But this principle—that personal, bodily acts (like sexual intercourse) only require one's moral commitments if one wants them to—has not stayed confined to abortion rights. Its prominent repetition through the years has caused it to become installed in the general public consciousness as an all-purpose—but very low grade—ethical standard for determining what one's moral duties are. So, women choose whether to become mothers, or more accurately, whether to give birth to the children they conceive. They choose whether or not to become mothers in the social sense. But men do not choose to become fathers. In fact, women—through electing either to obtain or not to obtain an abortion—choose *for* men whether men will become fathers (in the social sense), and whether men will be legally obligated to pay, over the course of nearly two decades, a substantial amount of money in child support.

The one-sidedness of this decision power is obvious.[57] Men's objections to it—which are rare because of the culturally required assent to "choice" and the intimidating feminist scorn which awaits any objection—are met with the retort, "Don't have intercourse if you're not ready to accept the duties of a father." But the same logic "Don't have intercourse if you're not ready to accept the duties of a mother" does not apply to women. They are allowed to choose whether or not to be a parent. Since men know that the woman they've impregnated could just as easily obtain an abortion as give birth to the child, they reason that if she foregoes the abortion—and they do not wish to assume the varied and sustained obligations of fatherhood—then the woman should have sole responsibility for the child. Why should I be responsible, he thinks, when she could have had an abortion? If she wants to choose to be a mother, that's fine for her, but she should not be able to influence my social and economic future by choosing for me whether I am to be a father.[58] My body, my choice. In fact, one man recently sued his lover for "misusing" his semen and becoming pregnant even though she told him she was using birth control. The man is refusing involvement in his child's life.[59]

So fatherhood, and the obligations attendant to it, are optional, just as motherhood, and the obligations attendant to it, are optional. Men have learned from the culture of "choice" that children's interests can be subjugated to their own personal desires, should the two conflict. Thus, our cultural enthroning of "choice" communicates to fathers, as it does to mothers, that children need not really be our top priority.

But beyond fomenting fatherlessness, "choice" has also worked to disengage men from their offspring, since their offspring don't socially become their offspring unless the woman wants them to. Hence, some men are psychologically ill-prepared to participate in raising their children once they are born, because they have suspended the development of a parental sense within themselves, obviously not wanting to experience the pain of having emotionally embraced their child only to lose him or her to abortion. Indeed, the sustained uncertainty that the possibility of abortion presents can even subtly turn a man's offspring into a menace in his own eyes, as its potential demise becomes the source of considerable anxiety. This uncertainty, plus the powerful cultural ascendancy of "a woman's right to choose," demotivates men from seeking to encourage the formation within themselves of emotional and psychological ties to their children. A man is understandably hesitant to embark down the personally profound road of fatherhood if he is unsure—and utterly powerless to establish—that his child will actually be born. I've known many men who didn't want their child aborted, but had no control over the situation, and so lost him or her.

So, many a man today has learned that the law of "choice" is a great wall separating him from his nascent children. Of course, had he not wished to be a father, this wall would have become a passageway to the abandonment of his most profound purpose as a man. How tragic it is that what is thought to be the empowerment of women—"choice"—at the same time discourages men from entering into fatherhood, and so contributes to the profound social corrosion wrought by fatherlessness. It is ridiculous indeed to believe that American society can restore a culture of responsible fatherhood while still tolerating the immoral rhetoric of "my body, my choice."

Conclusion

Can we honestly say today that our culture has not been coarsened and brutalized by the might-makes-right mentality of "My body, my choice"? January 23, 2000, marked the 27th anniversary of the day the U. S. Supreme Court unilaterally struck down the abortion laws of every state, and ignited a cultural conflagration. The flames still rage. It was an act of untempered judicial imperialism, and the decision immortalized as *Roe v. Wade* is widely regarded as a poorly reasoned and constitutionally unfounded opinion. But it lives on, not least because, as the court has progressively made clear in more recent rulings, most notably *Planned Parenthood v. Casey* (1992), the power of precedent and the social turmoil likely to result from its overrule are too great to countenance. But the regime of *Roe* itself is hardly a peaceful one, especially for the 35 million pre-born human beings whose lives it has violently claimed.

Eventually, the stress of the national delusion we have entered into regarding the inhumanity of the pre-born will become too much for our body politic to withstand. Just as on a personal level one lie always leads to other lies more difficult to sustain than the first, so it is socially. The fiction of a baby magically becoming a full human being at birth creates other inhumanities we loath to bear: gruesome partial-birth abortions, the brutal abandonment of newborns, pregnant women freely drinking alcohol (the leading cause of birth defects), and a train of other pathologies linked to the abortion license, from increased rates of breast cancer and sexually transmitted disease to the refusal of men to accept responsibility for paternity. And now, the horrific specter of cloning looms on the technological horizon. From human clones kept as insurance by the rich for failproof heart and liver transplants to clones simply auctioned off organ by organ, the anarchic abortion rationale, "My body, my choice," will be the anthem of justification for amorally prudent consumers and unethical scientific "providers." And for them, it is even stronger than for the "empowered" women of today, because, unlike those who abort, those who are cloned truly are operating on only their body, and no one else's.

No social order can encode into law the coarse contempt for nature and organic human relationships that is abortion on demand, and expect its fabric to remain intact. The unmatched love of a mother for her child has, throughout history, stood as the archetype of personal devotion and selflessness. It is nature's deepest bonding, and culture's highest calling. The abortion license turns mother against child, unleashes a perverse antagonism toward the unexpected or imperfect pre-born, and corrupts this most intimate of human affections.

In one of the post-*Roe* era's greatest ironies, the woman who pseudonymously gave the decision its petitioner's name gravely lamented its consequences in the most honest and, therefore, chilling terms: "[Women] have literally been handed the right to slaughter their own children." Can the land of the free withstand another 27 years of this debased liberty?

Chapter Five

THE PROBLEM WITH IMMIGRATION

Look, we're here now, we're not the minority, you are, so shut up!
—Hispanic activist, yelling at Jesse Peterson during a rally
protesting illegal immigration in Southern California.

The United States is, of course, a country of immigrants, built on the labor of immigrants—both voluntary and, in the horrific case of black slaves, forced. But it is one of the glories of our land that it has welcomed so many people from all points of confusion across the globe, and that for most of its history it has extended the opportunities of a lifetime to immigrants and their families. American generosity is beyond question, and it far outstrips that of any other nation, particularly those whose citizens flee in such prodigious numbers to our land.

But there is a problem today: in some parts of the country, particularly Southern California and South Texas, Hispanic immigration is so massive and culturally overwhelming, that it has disenfranchised poor American citizens, almost always black ones. Compounding this problem for black Americans in these areas, a significant percentage of this Hispanic immigration is illegal. This fact increases the frustration and dismay felt by many blacks, because they see the injustice of lawbreakers going unpunished, and non-Americans benefiting from the American system at black Americans' expense.

Of course, the extent of illegal immigration in these regions and elsewhere is notoriously difficult to ascertain, since government officers are afraid to investigate the matter for fear of being labeled by Hispanic activists as "racist," and since it is nonsensically against the law for public school districts to inquire about new enrollees' and their parents' immigration status (that is, whether they are legally or illegally in the country). But illegal immigration in Southern California has long been a concern of many citizens, and it led to the passage of the ultimately voided Proposition 187.[1] Conservatively, there are about 4 million Hispanic illegal immigrants in the U. S. today, the majority of them in Southern California, comprising the overwhelming balance of illegal immigration in that area.[2]

One indication of the scope of illegal Hispanic immigration in the L A. area comes from the city of Anaheim, 25 miles south of Los Angeles, which instituted, for a time, an immigration status checking service in its city jail. The city found in 1998 that nearly 1,000 inmates were illegal aliens, and that three of every ten inmates were foreign born, almost always Latino. Anaheim school board member Harold Martin, who is also a police officer in that city, says that consistently 37% of all arrestees in Anaheim are illegal immigrants.[3] The County of Orange, which includes Anaheim, has initiated a similar program for its jail, and took 4,472 illegal alien criminals into custody during 1998.[4] If only a modest percentage of illegal aliens commit other crimes, and if only a modest percentage of those are actually caught by law enforcement, given these figures one can get a general feeling for the profound extent of illegal immigration in Southern California. In fact, the problem of illegal aliens committing other offenses besides breaking into the country has become so pervasive, the United States Immigration and Naturalization Service has set up offices in several city jails around Southern California, to be able to more efficiently respond to the shocking volume of illegal aliens committing other offenses.

So, for the sake of resident Americans, to whom our nation has its first obligation, we must pursue sensible and fair immigration reform, and take seriously the legal identity of the American nation. The legislative details of the topic are far too complex for me to consider here, but I would simply like to emphasize the need for changes in the practice and enforcement of our immigration law. Basic fairness demands this. Massive immigration in concentrated areas is inconsistent with even the minimum American standard of life, and widespread illegal immigration—which is an undeniable reality—not only undermines the rule of law, it is also inhumane to illegal immigrants, permanently limiting their life chances in this country, trapping them in low wage jobs. And of course, the brain and labor drain on their homelands—usually Mexico—hinders those countries from improving themselves, and becoming economically self-sustainable.

My main concern though, in this chapter, is to emphasize the effect the huge recent influx of Hispanic immigrants in Southern California has had on black people. But first, I must point out that this is a topic almost completely undiscussed, for two general reasons. Black politicians and civil rights groups are all a part of the liberal coalition of grievance groups that includes the Hispanic rights organizations such as MALDEF (Mexican American Legal Defense and Education Fund), LULAC (League of United Latin American Citizrens), Mecha, Hermandad Mexicana Nacional and the National Council of La Raza. Therefore, these black groups observe a code of silence on this matter, even though black communities are, all over Southern California, up in arms over the transformation of their neighborhoods and schools, and lost job opportunities. Once again, black leadership has sacrificed the interests of the black public for their own political aggrandizement. It is more important to black leadership to follow the liberal party-line than to truly represent the sentiments of black citizens.

The second main reason little is ever said about the harm done to blacks because of the Hispanicization of Southern California is that the Hispanic Left has successfully used the race card to intimidate people into silence. To say what I have said so far, is assuredly to be called a "racist" by Hispanic rights groups. At a demonstration in which I participated at the Los Angeles Federal Building during the election debate over California's Proposition 187—which had it withstood court challenges after voter passage would simply have banned free government aid to illegal immigrants—everyone supporting the measure was denounced by those opposing the measure as "racists" and "bigots." A white man standing next to me was attacked by a bottle-wielding anti-187 hooligan, and needed first aid. But the coverage of that event and similar ones was sanitized by the local news, because the Hispanic establishment is very powerful in Los Angeles.[5]

Indeed, the news media and city and state governments are completely cowed into silence by the Hispanic race card, so there is no investigative reporting documenting the extent of illegal immigration, and, as I said, cities don't even require their school districts to inquire whether or not parents enrolling children in school are in the country legally. The power of the Hispanic race card is quite ironic: black public figures, who perfected calling others "racist" who disagreed with them, now are reluctant to voice their putative constituents' discontent with illegal immigration, in part for fear of being branded "racist" and losing their social standing as pure victims. But, of course, the Hispanic Left learned their trade from the black masters.

Tutelage in the Race Card

I've seen firsthand Hispanic immigrants' impressive commitment to 'making it' economically. But I'm convinced that these people, many of whom are first generation immigrants, are ill-served by Hispanic politicians and activists who claim to have their best interests in mind. Such politicians and community leaders would be wise to take a cue from the history and experience of the civil rights movement in this country and alter their style of advocacy.

In the years since the mid-sixties zenith of the civil rights movement, the continued political—as opposed to moral—emphasis of black advocacy has had a retarding effect on black life. Many of these effects I have analyzed earlier in these pages: Staggering teen pregnancy rates, a 25% rate of incarceration among young black males in California, and the obviously explosive feelings of frustration and rage felt throughout the urban poor. These all indicate a serious lack of progress over the last 30 years.

Indeed, a growing disparity in the black population—some move into the middle class, others stay mired in dysfunction—suggests, according to neighborhood activist Robert Woodson, a 'hustling' of poor blacks on the part of civil rights leaders eager to gain and secure the political capital that comes from representing a ruthlessly oppressed group.

Sadly, it seems this very same dynamic is at work in California—particularly Southern California—where the huge and rapidly growing Latino community is held out by Hispanic politicians and community groups as an increasingly victimized class, in need of government largesse and special social entitlement lest the bedlam visited upon Los Angeles in 1992 repeat itself. This misrepresentation—which seems to border on extortion—is accomplished mainly by citing figures showing Hispanics to be largely an impoverished segment of the population. This strategy usually works, of course, as we saw with the recent declaration (by a beaming Al Gore) of Santa Ana—a nearly total Hispanic city near Los Angeles bloated by huge immigration rates—a national "empowerment zone," and now heir to 100 million federal dollars over the next ten years.[6] Similarly, the Santa Ana Unified School District recently received a $600,000 federal grant for supplementary programs for students, again, by emphasizing students' underachieving and schools' overcrowded conditions, both the direct products of the immigration blitz.[7]

But it is a dishonest campaign, since the advocates fail to differentiate between the many brand new immigrants, who are often destitute, monolingual and uneducated—and other long time resident Hispanics who have progressed economically and assimilated culturally. Clearly nobody would expect, for example, poor Mexicans, newly emigrated, to be on an economic par with established residents. According to Linda Chavez's *Out of the Barrio*, 20 years ago the vast majority of Latinos were American born; today only about half of adult Latinos living in the United States were born here, and far less than that in areas like Southern California and South Texas. In light of this, it is inevitable that aggregate statistics on Latino economic standing—statistics skewed downward by the inclusion of a large number of new immigrants, frequently illegal—will not reflect the general well-being of Hispanic life.

But beyond this political subterfuge—and the resultant consumption of government resources some of which could have been allocated to black Americans' communities—Hispanic advocates have shown an uncritical willingness to enlist their constituency in the victim derby so prominent in American political discourse. For example, recent statements from the police chief of Orange, CA (he said rising crime rates in his city are mainly due to large numbers of illegal immigrants living there), and congressman Dana Rohrbacher (R, Huntington Beach, CA) (he said many of those arrested for looting during the '92 Los Angeles riots were illegal aliens, and should therefore be deported), have elicited from Hispanic politicians and activists outraged denunciations of (you guessed it) "racism" and "insensitivity." Dismissing both the possibility that what was said might be reasonable and, more significantly, the fact that they are empirical questions which can be proven true or false, Hispanic leaders instead chose to play the race card, mimicking the same style of group advocacy practiced for so long by the civil rights establishment. But these leaders seem unaware that not only is the political capital to be had from this approach wearing thin, it also encourages a race-consciousness among Hispanics that tends to have a paralyzing effect socio-economically, inclining those who hold it to embrace a discouraging and self-defeating victim-identity, and to look for extra-community political solutions to their problems.

Martin Luther King, Jr., said it was not a sign of weakness, but a sign of high maturity for a people to rise to the level of self-criticism. Those who would advance the welfare of Hispanics have—like black advocates before them—done their community a disservice by overlooking this principle of civic representation. The exclusively political thrust of Hispanic community activists leaves unattended the social pathologies that retard the economic mobility of any population—unwed pregnancies, single parent families, welfare dependency and crime rates. No immigrant group in the history of this country has ever progressed by majoring in the political. Group self-reliance and intra-group activism are the methods by which Hispanic leaders can best help immigrant Latinos attain the better life they are so obviously seeking.

Impact on Black Americans

The most disheartening effect on blacks of this immigration phenomenon is the conquest of black culture it entails. Cities in Southern California like Compton, Inglewood, Lynwood and South Central Los Angeles were not too long ago centers of black culture. Jazz clubs, soul food restaurants, and coffee shops catered to the local black clientele, and served as centers of community. Today, those places are long gone, and with them, the cultural deposits of black Californians have shrunk. It's hard for people in other parts of the United States to understand, but portions of Southern California have literally become more like Mexico than the United States. Part of this is because a great many Mexican immigrants retain strong identification with Mexico, so much so that to protest Proposition 187, they took to the streets waving Mexican flags, and, in some instances, burning American flags.[8] The hearts of many Mexican immigrants are still south of the border, as evidenced by the recent drive by some of the six to seven million Mexicans living in the U. S.—legally and illegally—to be allowed by Mexican law to vote, from the U. S. (usually California), in Mexican national elections. One poll found 83% of Mexicans living in America said they wanted to be able to vote in Mexican elections, without returning to Mexico.[9] Their hearts are still in Mexico, and for them America is merely a massive job-site, not a country to be cherished as one's own. Such Mexicans are very influential in Mexico, even though they live here, since they ship home five to seven billion American dollars *each year,* making them the third largest economic force in Mexico, after the petroleum and tourism industries.[10] Needless to say, this is five to seven billion dollars annually deleted from the United States economy, usually population centers with large black populations, since blacks and Hispanics often share neighborhoods.

But the transformation or conquest of neighborhoods is also, as I have said, simply a function of numbers. Recently the *Los Angeles Times* ran a series of stories about an entire Mexican village called El Granjanal, that emigrated to the Orange County city of Santa Ana. The entire town of 1,500 people moved to Santa Ana. This city of Santa Ana, the county seat of once notoriously white and Republican Orange County, has a population of about 330,000, one-third of a million. It is nearly 85% Hispanic, and a huge proportion of these residents are first generation immigrants. The student body of the school district—the fifth largest in California—is 91% Hispanic. The city is so solidly Mexican (not Mexican-American mind you, since proportionately few immigrants have had time to be naturalized, even if they are so inclined), that one Mexican street vendor casually explained to a reporter why people in his Santa Ana neighborhood were so ecstatic over Mexico's 1998 World Cup soccer win over South Korea: "This street is Mexico," Jose Rodriguez said, "Santa Ana is Mexico."[11]

Such comprehensive and swift demographic change is never civically healthy, and in a number of cities in Southern California this pattern of immigration is transpiring, and in the process culturally suffocating blacks.

Predictably, schools as well have been impacted, most prominently by bilingual education, which caters to—but disempowers—Hispanic students. How many thousands of black American kids have had their educational progress retarded, in part, at least, by the concurrent Spanish instruction in their classrooms? I have personally heard story after story at B.O.N.D. from frustrated black mothers enrolling their children in our after-school tutoring program, because these children have been unable to understand much of the instruction in their own classroom, because it was given in Spanish. Mercifully, bilingual education has for the most part ended, and, commonsensically, students in California are being taught in English.

Further, though, what about the lost job opportunities for blacks, particularly black youth? Often, that first summer job at McDonalds or after-school work at the local drug store gives critical lessons in responsibility for kids, and also provides valuable work experience. Those jobs have virtually all been absorbed by Hispanic immigrants. I know from personal experience that it is simply a lie that Americans, including black ones, will refuse to do low-wage work, and so, the story goes, that is the reason those jobs are filled by Hispanics. On the contrary, I know of many people, both personal friends and those who have come through the B.O.N.D. office searching for employment leads, who cannot obtain low-wage, service industry work because the workforce is saturated with Hispanic immigrants. Often, driving around town, I will see black men, most of whose families have been Americans for many, many generations, standing alongside groups of Hispanic men, waiting for day labor work. This seems inappropriate, that these longtime Americans would be on the same economic footing as those who perhaps just months ago were Mexican peasants. Certainly, the black men themselves must bear some substantial responsibility for being in that predicament, but with such a plentiful supply of low-wage labor in their cities, the availability to them of low-wage jobs becomes very scarce. And, as Barbara Jordan pointed out years ago, there is another subtle way in which large numbers of unskilled immigrants, as the huge balance of Hispanic immigrants are, harm the economic prospects of poor Americans, who are often black: these immigrants tend to accept lower wages and salaries (as well as fewer fringe benefits), when employers might be willing to pay higher, since they are glad just to have work. As Lawrence Harrison explains, this phenomenon "place[s] downward pressure on wages at the lower end that makes it more difficult for poor citizens to escape poverty."[12]

These realities, plus the general overcrowding and strain on civic services that the huge waves of immigrants in Southern California have fostered, have given rise to a palpable black-Hispanic hostility. The two races are alienated from each other, and they are in a very volatile relationship, living closely alongside each other. In fact, recently at a high school in Inglewood near Los Angeles, ethnic observances (black history month and Cinco de Mayo), had to be discontinued, because each year the inter-ethnic hostility between black and Hispanic students became more and more severe. Hispanic students felt insulted that only a day was given to celebrate their heritage (Cinco de Mayo), whereas black students had an entire month (February), to celebrate as Black History Month.

All of which is to say that, the madness of identity politics aside, we should not continue the way we are going with regard to immigration policy and practice. The untold dimension of the immigration debate in California and Texas is what Hispanicization is doing to the prospects of black Americans. This underreporting is, unfortunately, not likely to change, given the self-serving nature of black "leaders," and the complete cowardice of print and electronic journalists to face the local effects on blacks of Hispanic-dominated neighborhoods. As Xavier Hermosillo—Hispanic activist in Southern California and former talk radio host—is fond of saying to his black critics, in a dismissive jibe at the original civil rights movement, "You shall overcome, but we shall overwhelm!"

Chapter Six

THE PROBLEM WITH EDUCATION

Turn his mike off, turn his mike off! We don't have to listen to
this man come in here and criticize us!
> —*A Los Angeles Unified School Board member,*
> *responding to Jesse's call for educational reform.*

It doesn't take a genius to figure out that there is something seriously wrong with our public school system. Even though spending on public schools has gone up more than 200% since 1960,
SAT scores have declined 73 points.[1] A recent international math
and science study found that American 12th graders ranked 19th
out of 21 countries examined in mathematics, 16th of 21 in science, and 16th out of 16 countries studied in the field of ad-
vanced physics.[2] School discipline is notoriously bad. In 1940
American public school teachers said chewing gum, talking out
of turn and running in the hallways were their major disciplinary
problems. In 1990, public school teachers said the major disciplinary problems were drug and alcohol abuse, assault and pregnancy.[3] According to the U. S. Justice Department, 500,000 violent incidents a month are reported in the nation's public sec-
ondary schools, and each month 1,000 teachers need medical
treatment because of in-school assaults, and another 125,000 are
threatened.[4]

Meanwhile, our schools are teaching sex education, death education, the psycho-babble of self-esteem, and gay pride. The Los
Angeles Unified School District, the second largest in the nation and a monument to political correctness, even has "gay pride
month." There is not one day to honor America in that school

district, but they can spend a month taking instructional time to consider the merits of homosexuality.

I have spent untold hours sitting in public meetings of the L. A. School Board, and I marvel at how inefficient it is. This bureaucratic behemoth is an utter mess, and all too emblematic of the dysfunctional world of urban public education, in which so many black youth are trapped. Sixty-six percent of L.A. third graders cannot read at grade level; the dropout rate is more than twice the state average; SAT scores are about 13% below the state average, and sinking; district libraries have an average of five books per student, versus a national average of 20 per student; the school district spends nine percent more per pupil than the California average, yet only 60 cents of every dollar actually reaches the Los Angeles Unified classroom.[5] In a classic and mindboggling blunder, the L.A. Board of Education has poured $200 million into the downtown Los Angeles Belmont High School construction project (the most expensive in the nation), which sits atop a toxic wastesite, and is widely thought to be uninhabitable. At this point, it appears as though the site will have to be abandoned, and the money lost.

The simple fact is that the public school system in this country, particularly in inner cities, is a bureaucratic nightmare that clearly fails to educate children. As of 1990, only 56% of blacks over the age of 14 were able to read.[6] At B.O.N.D., one of our programs is free after school tutoring for kids, along with instruction in job-finding skills. On a regular basis, we have to teach high school seniors, usually black, how to read simple sentences, how to spell common words, how to fill out job application forms, and how to present themselves in an interview (dress well, be on time, say "please" and "thank you," don't use slang, etc.). The school system has failed these children miserably. The back-to-basics movement is gaining strength among the black population, especially poor blacks, because they are seeing that the failures of the public educational system are hurting their children's lifechances, and holding them back.

The Voucher Solution

This is why so many black families, and minorities generally, support the school-choice, or school vouchers, movement. Such programs simply return to parents the money for educating their children the government takes from them in the form of taxes, and allows the parents to choose where to enroll their child and spend their education dollar. One recent survey found that 72% of black Americans favor vouchers so their kids will be able to attend private schools.[7] Another survey found that almost 80% of the inner city poor favored vouchers.[8] When the Children's Scholarship Fund offered partial scholarships to inner city children (essentially a privatized voucher program), there were 1.25 million applications for 40,000 awards.[9]

The reasons for this support are obvious: inner city parents cannot both pay taxes *and* afford private school for their kids, and their public schools are violent cesspools of drugs, profanity, disorder, harried teachers and poor instruction. These parents want their children out of such environments, and they know that private schools will provide more effective discipline for their children, successfully teach them basic academic skills, and better motivate them to excel. Voucher schools are almost always smaller than public schools, and this lower teacher-to-student ratio has obvious educational value. It reduces student tension and alienation, and promotes a sense of accountability and therefore responsibility among students.[10] Private schools, as schools of choice, are often more stimulating and nurturing for students because they are free of the bureaucratic red tape so common with public schools, and are therefore free to design more creative and innovative curriculums that can provide a rigorous, holistic education for students, touching their mind and soul.[11] And, from the larger public's standpoint, private schools are a better buy for the dollar. Study after study has confirmed that poor kids do better—for less per pupil cost—in private than in public schools. Vouchers would actually end up saving the public money.

There is also a simple, but powerful, moral logic to the case for vouchers. Everyone financially supports public schools through transfer payments (taxes), and they do this out of legal compulsion. It is only fair that parents—who love their children more than the government does, and who have a primary, natural responsibility for them—have the option to spend that portion of their taxes designated for their children's education on the educational experience they themselves choose for their children. This is only fair.[12] Parents, not the state, should make the decision about how the parent's children are to be educated. The logic of voucher programs recognizes the preeminence of the family in social order, and it takes authority out of the hands of educrats and so-called "experts," and puts it back in the hands of parents, who can then manage their child's education themselves. This is morally beautiful, and a critically important reason why people concerned about the authority of the family being undermined by government should speak out in favor of school choice.

Yet, by forbidding vouchers, the government takes educational expenses from parents and itself chooses where and how to spend that money, leaving parents—a portion of whose income has been confiscated for the education of their child—quite possibly unable to afford placing their child in the school of their own choice (a private religious school, perhaps).

The hypocrisy of liberal voucher opponents is really stunning. Seventy percent of the Congressional Hispanic Caucus and 30% of the Congressional Black Caucus send their children to private schools, yet they both completely oppose vouchers for the Hispanic and black poor, so their children can go to private schools.[13] The Clintons and the Gores—not to mention Jesse Jackson himself—all sent their children to fine private schools, not the often terrifying public schools of Washington, D.C. Yet, along with the education lobby, by opposing vouchers they forbid the poor black families of Washington, D.C. to share in the chance to send their children to cleaner, safer, better managed private schools.[14] These liberals, white and black, are in league with the teachers' unions which oppose vouchers because they don't want competition. Neither group is open-minded enough to seriously consider conservative ideas like voucher plans. As journalist

Matthew Miller says, "To listen to the [teachers'] unions and the NAACP, one would think that vouchers were the evil brainchild of the economist Milton Friedman and his conservative devotees...."[15]

The depth to which Black "leadership" is out of step with the black public on vouchers is hard to comprehend. It is profound. Robert L. Woodson well describes the disconnect between black civil rights professionals and the black public on the issue of school vouchers. He writes: "In one survey sponsored by Home Box Office, Inc., and conducted by the Joint Center for Political and Economic Studies, 83% of black respondents who knew about school vouchers said they were in favor of choice programs "where parents can send their children to any public or private school that will accept them." Yet, in a floor vote at the 1993 NAACP convention, delegates passed a resolution opposing voucher programs that would provide low-income children with the means to attend private schools."[16]

Furthermore, although liberals vocally support integration in schools, they oppose vouchers, a great tool of integration. Vouchers would clearly place more blacks in private schools which are overwhelmingly white. For example, in Manhattan, the capital of American politically-correct liberalism, public schools are 90% minority, while private schools are 80% white.[17] But not even the chance to realize what they say is one of their greatest goals can entice self-serving black and white liberals to break step with the teachers' unions and education lobbies.

A Hard Road

But the task facing potential voucher schools in inner cities is a daunting one. *In the Classroom,* a 1997 book detailing author Mark Gerson's teaching experience in a mostly black private school in urban New Jersey, is an insightful example of how great the educational challenges will be for voucher schools, challenges primarily due to the deep scarring caused by value-free public education and race-conscious rhetoric in black communities.

Gerson paints a realistic and disturbing picture of inner-city culture. The profanities constantly flying from students' mouths—both in class and out—would make a Navy Seal blush, and their manipulativeness (often exemplified by calling their teacher a "racist" in an attempt to avoid homework or detention) is unrelenting.

Indeed, it is on the subject of race and racism that Gerson's book is especially sobering, at least for those people unaware of the depth and intensity of black racism. The mostly black inner-city students demonstrate a virulent anti-white prejudice. Main sources of their discontent are the hip-hop culture in which they are immersed, the obsession with conspiratorial speculation that permeates their neighborhoods, and race-baiting celebrities like Al Sharpton and Louis Farrakhan, in whose anger the students exult.

Thus, Gerson encounters an assortment of bizarre sentiments, as when a young black student thinks Oreo cookies should no longer be sold in the school cafeteria because the cookies are "racist." How does she know this? "Because it is two blacks crushing the white. It is meant for whites to be scared of blacks. That's why whites take the Oreos apart, so they can eat a black without eating a white. Ever see a white person eating the white part?"[18] Who enlightened this black teenager to this sinister reality? A teacher she had when she was enrolled in the local public high school.

Other manifestations of the students' sad and perverse certainty whites hate them include: the unshakable belief in O. J. Simpson's innocence (just 4 out of Gerson's 120 students thought Simpson guilty), the negative racial implications of a teacher's shirt or pen color, and the inscrutable ability of the police to frame famous black men who have run afoul of the law (Simpson, Mike Tyson, Marion Barry, Daryl Strawberry, and the late Tupac Shakur).

All of which points to this undeniable reality about the public schools in inner cities: they teach racial hostility and racial separatism to black kids. From African-American pride celebrations, and the ridiculous rumors about whites, the atmospheres in these schools teach black kids to focus on color, not character. This teaching of ethnic pride and race-consciousness is immensely harmful to children. Black pride won't get them a job; learning fables about how great Africa was won't get kids onto the corporate ladder today.

Citizens of good will all across America must insist on school vouchers so poor blacks and other low-income people can have a chance to give their kids a decent education, one that can overcome the angry, demotivating and intellectually disabling culture of urban black life.

The Bitter Fruit of Anti-White Feelings: "Acting White"

Perhaps the clearest evidence today of black racism, and of the terrible harm blacks are doing to their own children's futures by teaching them to hate whites (as we see some of Gerson's students certainly do), is the charge of "acting white" often leveled by black students at their high-achieving peers whom, perversely, they wish to denigrate.[19] For some time now, black students have used the hatred against whites that is in their communities as a way to bully academically gifted black peers into conforming to the academic mediocrity around them.

The charge "acting white" has the force it does because white people are generally despised in black communities.[20] Therefore, any trait ascribed to them—like diligence in school, bookishness, cooperating with authority—is likewise contemptible. Of course, since these are the main habits that make for a successful education, the "acting white" charge, and its intimidating threat, dooms many black kids to underachievement in school. In this way, black racism creates an ethic of anti-achievement in black communities.[21] To get a feeling for how the "You're acting white" insult functions, read the following excerpt from a report dealing with the subject by Charles Gibson on the television news magazine 20/20.[22]

Gibson: "Katie Jones is a history and ethnic studies teacher at East High School. Underachieving black students, she says, will prey on the achievers."

Katie Jones: "Those kids who work very hard, who take pride in pleasing a teacher in terms of the assignments, getting the work done, doing what is expected of any student—that student, unfortunately, will deal with students that seem to think they've simply sold out."

Charles Gibson: "…[A]ccusations [of acting white] can hurt so much that some [black] students will consciously underperform in class to avoid them."

Black Female Student: "I wouldn't like, answer all the questions that I knew was right, you know. I had just probably like slouched back in my chair and be like, you know, like this or something [slouching]. And I wouldn't answer questions."

Another Black Female Student: "I used to get straight As all the time. There was this girl who's like, 'Dang, she's acting white. Look at you. You just a goodie two shoes.' And like everywhere I went, she'd call me a goodie two shoes. So I end up dropping my grades, just like doing bad on like a couple of tests so she'd leave me alone. I got Cs on them. But I couldn't pull my grades back up after that."

This kind of behavior from black kids is an unspeakable tragedy, yet it happens among black students hundreds of times each school day, at public schools all across the country. It is patterns of behavior like this, not white racism, that is retarding the education of black children. But Hell will freeze over before the great "black leaders" of our time address this problem. Interior problems like this, problems inside the black community itself, are uninteresting to them, because there is no white guilt to be manipulated, and therefore no political advantage to be gained from them.

An Inevitable Victory

Partly because of the detestable culture of black public education described above, the voucher movement is steadily growing, and it is only a matter of time until it escapes from under the foot of the civil rights and education establishments, and demonstrates its potential. Besides all the persuasive theoretical and practical reasons, I believe it will be the personal testimonies of joyful parents and transformed children that finally become the decisive force in the inevitable victory of school voucher programs over the educational status quo. Consider the following testimony of the power of school vouchers, presented by columnist Armstrong Williams:

> "I feel that [school vouchers] literally saved my daughter's life," explained Nicky Cavanaugh, a single mother who was able to switch her daughter to a private school with the help of a Florida voucher program. Cavanaugh said that her fifth grade daughter, Stacy, was so terrorized by stabbings, theft and other random acts of violence that every morning the little girl begged and cried not to return. Getting accepted into the school voucher program provided a way out. "You know, since we got the scholarship, it gave us the opportunity for a new life," Cavanaugh said.[23]

Chapter Seven

WHAT AMERICANS SHOULD DO NOW

We are where we are because whenever we had a choice to make, we have chosen the alternative that required the least effort at the moment....[We] have dissipated, like wastrels and drunkards, the inheritance of freedom and order that came to [us] from hardworking, thrifty, faithful, believing, and brave men.
*—Journalist Walter Lippmann, on the
eve of American involvement in WWII*

If you keep doing what you've been doing, you keep getting what you got.
—Robert L Woodson, Sr.

America is unique. It is the only country built on values, not ethnicity. If we return to the American values of diligence, self-control, and real belief in God we can return this country to the shining city on a hill we all know it was meant to be, and we can live like genuine men, independent and self-sufficient.
—Jesse Lee Peterson, addressing a gathering of young black men.

As the new millennium begins, all Americans are faced with a question: will we continue to allow the cultural domination of amoral liberalism to transform our society into a selfish contest over which group is recognized as the greatest historical victims, which group should receive legal preferences, and which group will have their "rights" more fully respected?

As a nation we are rushing toward the empty freedom from responsibility. But this frantic flight is hopelessly misguided. True liberty, true emancipation, and true autonomy come first from self-control, and then from the self-government and the self-

sufficiency to which it leads. The corrupt understanding of freedom today—that it simply means doing whatever you want to
do, without any moral restraint—is not only unfulfilling and un-
satisfying to people, it also leads to the bondage of addiction and
hedonism. Real satisfaction is found in serving others, first and
foremost your family. We have lost this realization today, and
seek to minimize our responsibilities, thinking this will give us
more freedom. In fact, all it ends up doing is shrinking our souls,
and isolating us from other people.

What is the path back to a strong national culture again? How
can America again become an internally strong country, and not
just a militarily strong country? I believe the answer is plain: we
must focus again on the family, learn to be grateful for being
Americans, and recover the knowledge we once had that no nation
can survive without emphasizing public moral standards.

Back to the Family

One of most disturbing phenomena since the 1960s has been
the steady erosion of the authority of the family. Whether through
no-fault divorce, the deregulation of sexual morality, the homosexual rights movement, the endless liberal propaganda about
the virtues of daycare or the feminist ethic of women working
whether they are mothers or not—whether they financially need
to or not—the family as the center of our lives has diminished in
importance. Under the dominance of contemporary liberalism,
government programs, daycare, and the pursuit of self-fulfillment
have replaced the family as the focal point of individual experience. In fact, today, there is among the liberal elite an outright
hostility toward the traditional family. The recent outrage over
an all-female college's brochure proudly stating that women who
attend all-female schools marry and have children at a higher
rate than women who attend co-ed schools is a case in point.
The college had to amend the flier, because so many liberal activists were offended at the exaltation of marriage and children
as life's ideal.[1]

Indeed, today any arrangement of people living together—married or not, homosexual or heterosexual—is considered of equal value with the traditional nuclear family. When ideas like this prevail, it is no wonder there are so many unhappy, broken homes and families.

The basic problem here is a failure to rightly understand human nature, and the order of human society. I've often said that liberalism is a battle against human nature, and, when it comes to the family policies advocated by the Left today, I think that is especially clear.

Men and women both have a natural desire to bond with one another, and form families. That is the way God has constructed us. Deep within each of us is the awareness that we were meant to give ourselves to others, and to contribute to the flourishment of humanity by caring for the next generation. The best way to do this is in the context of the traditional family. This is what is best for children (the support of a mother and a father), and this is what yields the greatest depth of human satisfaction. There is no one more content than an old, married couple, a man and a woman who have been with one another throughout life's ups and downs, and who have shared together the most intimate moments of humanity.

The Bible tells us that the family is God's invention, and that it is the basic foundation of society, the root of civilization. When families break down, social order breaks down, and everyone suffers as a result. Consider these recent developments in American family life:

• In 1960, 5% of all births were out-of-wedlock; by the early 1990s, one third of all births were out-of-wedlock.[2]

• By the year 2000, 40% of all American births and 80% of minority births will be out-of-wedlock.[3]

• About one fourth of all unwed women in the United States become unwed mothers.[4]

• Since 1960, the percentage of American families headed by a single parent—usually a woman—has more than tripled.[5]

• The national divorce rate has more than doubled since

1960.[6]

• Each year, more than one million children in this country have parents who separate or divorce.[7]

• The United States has the highest divorce rate in the world.[8]

The social hardships of tomorrow are the products of the family failures of today. In order to lessen the wave of social pathology that threatens to swamp us in the next few decades (from increased rates of illegitimately to male criminality to simply angry, hostile young adults), we must recognize that the primary responsibility every person has is to make certain they have a stable, emotionally secure family. This is the orderly way to build the strength of a society, by first building the strength of its families. People need to realize that they may have to forego the high-powered career to raise their children, they may have to drive only one car instead of two, have one TV instead of two, or live in a small house instead of a bigger house. All this, and more, so that there can be one parent home with the kids, ensuring their emotional and physical well-being.

We have to start sacrificing for our kids again. We used to do that, but the cultural revolution of the 1960s took that away from us. We need to know that when children are number one, and family life surpasses all our other concerns, we are acting most in line with our nature, and we are fulfilling our most critical responsibilities. Plus, given the reality of family dysfunction today, we are contributing to nothing less than the redemption of our society.

Gratitude to God and Country

Gratitude is an idea out of fashion today. The religion of self-esteem has taught us to believe we deserve all the good things we have, and then some. To humbly acknowledge thanksgiving for good fortune is thought to imply personal weakness, and a lack of self-esteem. But this is a profoundly mistaken way of thinking. Besides greatly overvaluing the importance of self-esteem, it removes from people one of the best and most effective ways they can achieve happiness and stability for their lives and for their country, and that is through gratitude.

Gratitude is a deep sense of gratefulness for the opportunities and goods one has. Gratitude, if regularly practiced, becomes a habit of mind that lends a peacefulness to our lives that we cannot have if we believe we must constantly strive and earn whatever good we have.

The fact is, the greatest blessing we Americans have is America itself, and this is not something of our making; it is something given to us by the founding fathers and by the Judeo-Christian moral tradition on which our country is based. Americans today don't spend enough time thinking about how wonderful their country is, and how much it has given to all of us. People in other countries, ironically, understand how exceptional a country the United States is, which is why so many of them want so desperately to emigrate here. The American experiment in self-government has been a stunning success so far, and we all should be profoundly thankful for that.

American Keith Richburg, *Washington Post* correspondent, discovered the unique greatness of this country when he was based in Africa. His memoir, *Out of America,* is an important illustration of why everyone who lives in this country, including, or perhaps I should say especially, blacks, are so fortunate to be here.

Throughout Richburg's tour of duty in Africa he shows us not only the famines and massacres that make international news, but also the brutal culture of inhumanity that grips everyday life: the abuses of basic human rights and trampling of liberties by tribal dictators, the police harassment, random beating and imprisonment of political dissidents, the firebombing of newspapers which dare oppose the local strongman, and the outright murder of anyone forthrightly condemning these patent injustices. And it is this suppression of virtuous reformers by maniacal warlords and petty despots that chains much of Africa to the bleakest of futures. As Richburg notes: "In Africa, the good guys don't win; they usually get tossed in prison, tortured, killed, beaten up, or sometimes just beaten down. They get beaten so hard they finally give up. And the rest? They just stop trying because they're too busy simply trying to survive."[9]

Indeed, surviving is a formidable task for most everyone in the largely lawless sub-Sahara. If they escape starvation or pestilence, they must still fear the machete or ubiquitous AK-47, weapons often wielded by young teenagers high on marijuana or *khat*, a stimulating weed chewed like tobacco. The gruesome and perverse scenes powerfully presented by Richburg clearly convey the horror and nihilism that is so common to the area. For example:

• The butchered bodies of Tutsi Rwandans floating down the Kagera River into Tanzania, one crossing the border every 30 seconds for more than two days. Their now bloated, discolored corpses were mutilated by Hutu tribesmen, resentful of Tutsi rule and ethnic difference.

• In comparatively civilized Nairobi, Kenya, a teenage boy is screaming in terror as he is held to the ground by several men. One of his hands has already been chopped off, and the older man standing above him wielding a large knife is poised to hack off the other, as an interested crowd gathers to casually witness the gore. The boy had been caught stealing.

• Liberia's ruinous civil war is as bizarre as it is destructive: former Boston gas station attendant Charles Taylor, now a rebel leader, controls much of the country, including a section he has christened "Taylorland." In the perpetual skirmishes between warring factions, combatants wear women's wigs, pantyhose, and Halloween masks, all often covered with mud in the belief that it will protect them from their enemies' bullets.

A telling irony is experienced by Richburg in his travels throughout Africa: it is the fact he is an American, not a black man, that provides him some protection and respect. In the constant border and customs checks he is subjected to by self-important soldiers and bureaucrats (a pathetic paradox since the "governments" they represent are in constant disarray), his American passport shields him from being supposed a tribal infiltrator. Similarly, in South Africa, when a white woman brazenly cut in front of him in a supermarket line, his protest in an American midwestern twang drew from the woman a flustered and red-faced, "I'm sorry, I thought you were African!"

Richburg went to Africa hoping to have an epiphany of sorts, to feel an intense kinship with his ancestors, and to recognize the centrality of his race to his personality. But in the end, he realizes he must look within himself to understand who he is, and not to some mythic African paradise.[10] He writes, "[W]hile I know that 'Afrocentrism' has become fashionable for many black Americans searching for identity, I know it cannot work for me. I have been here, I have lived here and seen Africa in all its hor-ror. I know now that I am a stranger here. I am an American, a black American, and I feel no connection to this strange and violent place."[11]

Thus, despite all the mind-numbing murder and epic degra-dation of human life Richburg unflinchingly relates, emerging out of his record is the individualistic and ultimately humanizing realization that human identity utterly transcends tribe and race, and that the threads of civilization easily fray when this truth is ignored.

As Richburg's brilliant narrative shows, suffering is far greater all around the globe than it is here. That is one reason why the whining and rage of the black middle class is so nonsensical. They simply don't know how great they have it. This is the least racist country of any, and yet, that's virtually all so many black people talk about, while completely blind to their own racism.

Gratefulness for being an American will give calm and peace to anyone. Our good fortune to be born on this soil, or to have emigrated here, is something we should regularly dwell on, and openly thank God for. Sometimes before a meal, rather than say a prayer of thanks for the food, I will say a prayer of thanks that I live in America, and that I am an American. This kind of con-stant thankfulness for our nation will give us a stable mental outlook toward society, and it will also help us to see our own lives in the context of history and the struggles of others, struggles often much greater than our own.

But even more vital than sincere appreciation for our decent country, is thankfulness to God for the gift of life itself. When is the last time you said, "Thank you God, for giving me life; thank you, for letting me live"? This kind of meditation is extremely important, because it acknowledges our personal subservience to God, and our dependence upon him. This is important to do, because it puts us in agreement with the order of the universe. We are not higher than God, we are not capable of self-sustenance without him. As simple as it is, it is critical that we acknowledge that.

As the first stanza in Johnson Oatman, Jr.'s song *Count Your Blessings* reminds us:

> When upon life's billows you are tempest tossed,
> when you are discouraged, thinking all is lost,
> count your many blessings, name them one by one,
> and it will surprise you what the Lord hath done.

Thankfulness to God cultivates dependence on him, and this is good, because that is why we were created, to trust in him and to worship him. When we act in line with our ultimate purpose as human beings, we experience personal satisfaction and happiness.

Sadly, in our country today, we don't really take God seriously. Oh yes, there is a lot of church chat on TV, a lot of religious programming, and a lot of televangelists still proclaiming their need for our "love gift," that is, our money. But despite all of this religious rhetoric, we as a people haven't genuinely submitted ourselves to God and his rule.[12] This is obviously the case, because if we had, we wouldn't be experiencing the cultural breakdown we are, and the assault of immorality that is plainly around us. Self is our new god, and we will allow nothing to compete with it.

This is a shame, because apart from God, we are not going to be truly content or satisfied. There is, within each of us, a longing for God, a hunger for ultimate truth, and until we give our lives to him, and show our love for God by being obedient to his moral law written on our hearts, we will not grow into the kind of people he wants us to be, the kind of people who do what's right for its own sake, the kind of people who are in the habit of being responsible, and who have the integrity to urge others around them to be the same way.

Public Moral Standards

The third general change of course we must make if we are to recover personal peace and social stability is to once again establish virtue as an honorable and attainable goal for human behavior. Today the concept of virtue is snickered at, and regarded as nothing more than an uptight personality flaw, or outright intolerance.

But unless we recover the vision of human virtue that once prevailed in this country, we will not have a roadmap for our behavioral recovery. What are the virtues we should hold up for our children to aspire to? Rather than just bury them in condoms, and teach them to surrender to their urges, we should teach them to respect their bodies, and be sexually pure. Rather than allow them to yield to selfishness, we should teach them that they ought to care about other people, and treat everyone the way they themselves wish to be treated. Rather than permitting them to curse and be rude, and treat adults like children, we should insist they have a civil tongue, and treat all adults with deferential respect. Children will rise—or sink—to the level of expectations given them. If we love our children, we should expect much from them.

These are not radical ideas. They are the common sense ethic that this country was built on, and the moral minimum that responsible people should meet. Yet, one of the reasons we do not require it of our children, or expect it of the adult population at large, is that we have completely accepted the liberal definition of compassion, which is, simply, let people do whatever they want. To the liberal mind, expecting people to be virtuous is mean and intolerant, because it indicates you are making judgments about people's conduct, and asserting some choices are better than others, and ought to be selected.

But what the hyper-emotional liberal mind doesn't realize is that high behavioral expectations of people are a sign of respect and concern for them, not indifference and contempt. If you want to help someone, you will honestly tell them their mistakes. If you care about somebody, you will consistently hold them to high ethical standards. If you are compassionate to people, you will not excuse their wrongdoing, but fairly name it, and speak to them of the importance of following a tried and true moral code that can bring stability and success to their life.

The confused conception of compassion in modern liberalism is that nice, tolerant people will allow others to make whatever "lifestyle choices" they wish, without telling them whether what they have done and the habits they are thereby forming are right or wrong, personally edifying or personally corrupting. This is not genuine compassion. Contemporary liberalism has replaced the moral vocabulary of Judeo-Christian ethics with the therapeutic slogans of narcissistic culture, in which desires matter more than obligations, intentions more than actions, and feelings more than character.

This inversion of moral order has led to the denunciation of those who insist on the possibility and necessity of public virtue. "Bigot" and "Right-wing fanatic" are the usual epithets. But the ad hominems the Left so regularly issues to its conservative critics only show how intellectually bankrupt it is.

Is it so radical to believe that we can do what is right? Is it really so bizarre to believe that our families should be the center of our lives? Is it unreasonable to be grateful to God for America, and the incredible blessings it has bestowed on people from all around the world? I don't think so, on all counts, and I think that the social greatness of the Land of the Free can be restored by a public journey back to common decency, and by a personal journey back to self-responsibility.

I know from the experience of my own life that people can change. Anger can be overcome, responsibility can be realized, peace of mind can be achieved. May God help all of us to forgive those who have hurt us in the past, to honor him in the present, and to rest in him for the future.

Appendix I

A Declaration of Racial Commonsense

The hardest activity in human life is to love the stranger. We all tend to be wary of those who are different from us, whether those differences be religious, cultural or racial. Yet, it is undeniably a necessary prerequisite for any just society that we resist this inclination, and that people not be judged by what they look like. Rather, they must be judged by how they act.

Martin Luther King, Jr., stated it with simple eloquence and moral power when he adjured us to treat each other on the basis of the content of our character, and not the color of our skin. Too often this phrase is dismissed as only platitudinous, but it has yet to truly be tried in this country. We wholeheartedly affirm this simple but essential ethical imperative, and recommend it anew to our rending national fabric. We must know each other as we are, and interact on that basis alone, not according to how we imagine one another to be, or to how politically self-serving special interest groups portray those different from us.

We must recall and recite the humanizing and politically emancipating lesson learned by the great Jewish psychiatrist and writer Viktor Frankl, who upon emerging from the horrors of Auschwitz, said that there were really only two groups of people in this world: the decent and the indecent. The ethnic cheerleading and group-identification that dominates American politics today is the absolute opposite of this principle, and ought to be completely rejected by men and women of goodwill.

To all but the most stubborn utopians it long ago became apparent that one of the greatest hindrances to the fostering of social cooperation is human nature itself. James Madison put it well when he said "If men were angels, no government would be necessary." Human beings are capable of great and redemptive acts, but the record of history makes it undeniable that they are also capable of great evil. Racism is one of those evils. We humbly affirm this, and call for an end to resentment and ethnic chauvinism—on the part of all Americans—and for a return to the common sense knowledge that unless each of us guards his or her own heart and mind, we too could enter into the poison quicksand of racial animosity, which accomplishes nothing of worth, but only feeds the ugly part of human nature, and in the process debases the quality of society as a whole.

Human beings can only flourish if they know that their best efforts will not go unrewarded, and that there is a very strong relationship between personal effort and individual achievement. We affirm that essential to imparting this confidence to people is strict and overt political equality. The vitality of American democracy rests upon the willingness of policy makers and the general public to insist that individual people be held responsible for their own individual behavior. The law must treat all citizens the same, irrespective of their race. Legally and politically, we must not give place to any distinctions based solely in skin color or cultural heritage. To its great shame, this country once did. But it must no more. We must rise to the level of our ideals, and insist that the law be absolutely color-blind, and that we pursue genuine political equality by refraining from codifying into law racial or gender preferences of any sort. This will oblige us to pursue the empowerment of the less fortunate by other means, notably the promotion of the community-building work of voluntary associations and the ferocious enforcement of anti-discrimination laws. If the dis-uniting of America is to cease, people of conscience must step up and declare that our national vitality will not be siphoned off either by petty bigotries or by the self-indulgent politics of grievance groups, who continually rush to stake their self-regarding and cynical claim in the political klondike of victimization.

The United States today is at a racial crossroads. We can continue down the jarring path of group identification, with its wounding rhetoric and inherent hostility, or we can turn toward racial common sense, with its individualist ethic and emphasis on personal responsibility. We urge the latter course, in the hopes of the widespread recognition of the simple truth which regrettably few pluralistic cultures ever comprehend, a truth which has been tragically eclipsed by the collectivist politics of today: we are more alike than we are different, more human than we are racial.

Endorsees:
(Participation by endorsees does not necessarily indicate agreement with the opinions or ideas expressed in the text of *From Rage to Responsibility*. Institutional affiliations are listed for identification purposes only).

Rev. Jesse Lee Peterson
President, B. O. N. D.

Brad Stetson
Director, The David Institute

Shelby Steele
The Hoover Institution

Robert L. Woodson, Sr.
President, National Center for
Neighborhood Enterprise

Errol Smith
Vice-Chair, California Civil
Rights Initiative

Clint Bolick
Litigation Director,
Institute for Justice

Walter E. Williams
George Mason University

Ken Hamblin
Nationally Syndicated Columnist

Dennis Prager
Co-Director, Empower America

Niger Innis
National Spokesperson, C. O. R.E.

David Almasi
Director, Project 21

Ward Connerly
Chief Spokesman,
California Civil Rights Initiative

Appendix II

American Organizations and Publications Supportive of Black Conservatism

The American Enterprise Institute does research on race and American politics, and publishes the very helpful bimonthly "The American Enterprise" magazine. Obtain information on AEI from 1150 17th St. NW, Washington, DC 20036.

Americans For Family Values directed by Ezola Foster, is a Southern California-based organization that deals with family issues. For more information, write to Americans For Family Values, 2554 Lincoln Blvd., #264, Venice, CA 90291.

The Brotherhood Organization of a New Destiny (B.O.N.D.) is directed by Jesse Lee Peterson. B.O.N.D. is a non-profit self-help organization dedicated to neighborhood empowerment and helping young black men grow into maturity. The mailing address is P. O. Box 35090, Los Angeles, CA 90035—0090. Their internet address is www.bondinfo.org .

Center for New Black Leadership seeks to revive and encourage traditional solutions to social and economic problems in the African-American community. The Center advocates ideas and institutions that are consistent with the black community's long held commitments to individual initiative and personal responsibility. For more information, contact The Center for New Black Leadership at 733 15th Street, NW, Suite 700, Washington, DC 20005.

Center for the Study of Popular Culture is directed by David Horowitz, and publishes *Heterodoxy*, a chronicle of cultural and media trends. Their address is 12400 Ventura Blvd., Studio City, CA 91604.

The David Institute is a Southern California-based research group that is dedicated to the defense of human dignity. The David Institute is strongly supportive of black conservatives. For information, write to The David Institute, P.O. Box 1248, Tustin, CA 92781.

Heritage Foundation is a conservative public policy research organization, located at 214 Massachusetts Ave. NE, Washington, DC 20002. They publish *Policy Review*, and frequently cover the topics of race and racial politics.

Institute for Contemporary Studies is an independent Bay Area public policy research organization emphasizing the necessity and virtue of self-government. Write for information on their publications and projects to 1611 Telegraph Avenue, Suite 902, Latham Square, Oakland, CA 94612.

Institute for Justice, directed by Clint Bolick, is a leading supporter of school voucher programs and neighborhood empowerment. Contact them at 1717 Pennsylvania Ave., NW, Suite 200, Washington, DC 20006.

Institute on Religion and Public Life is directed by Richard John Neuhaus and publishes the important and elite monthly journal *First Things.* Subjects addressed in this eclectic publication range from the liberal assault on the Judeo-Christian tradition to the dignity of the individual. Write to them at 156 5th Avenue, Suite 400, New York, NY 10010.

Issues and Views is edited by Elizabeth Wright, and is an absolutely indispensable forum for black conservative thought and social criticism. Published quarterly, it is available from Elizabeth Wright, P. O. Box 467, New York, NY 10025.

The Lincoln Review is edited by J. A. Parker, and is an important and venerable journal of black conservative analysis. Obtain information from The Lincoln Institute, 1001 Connecticut Ave. NW, Suite 1135, Washington, DC 20036.

The National Center for Neighborhood Enterprise (NCNE) is directed Robert Woodson, Sr. It is a non-profit organization operating many programs helping lower income black Americans achieve self-sufficiency and financial independence. Write to the National Center for Neighborhood Enterprise at 1367 Connecticut Avenue, NW, Washington, DC 20036.

The National Center for Public Policy Research (NCPPR) is a research organization that administers Project 21, a black leadership organization. Project 21 is a networking group that publicizes the views of black conservatives. Information about Project 21 is available from Project 21 at 300 Eye Street, NE, Suite 3, Washington, DC 20002.

Reconcilers magazine is an excellent publication which features family-centered black advocacy and racial reconciliation. It highlights the efforts of the Christian Community Development Association. *Reconcilers* magazine is available from 1909 Robinson Street, Jackson, MS 39209.

Notes

Chapter Two: The Problem with Race

1. See the column by A. S. Doc Young, "Negatives and Positives," *The Los Angeles Sentinel,* November 14, 1991.

2. Dennis Prager, "Why Have Race and Ethnicity Become So Important?" *The Prager Perspective,* June 15, 1996, p. 3.

3. This survey data was widely reported, here it is drawn from William F. Buckley, Jr., "Black/White—What's What?," *National Review,* September 28, 1998, pp. 66-67.

4. "Thomas spends time off in public eye," *USA Today,* October 5, 1998, p. 4A.

5. The role of white elite liberals in inflaming social anger at large is woefully underexamined. A typical case in point though, no doubt serving as a model for advocacy groups of all kinds in how to express rage, is Alan Dershowitz's creed against the "radical right," "anti-environmentalism," conservative Christianity, and the right to life movement—the elements of American conservatism he faults for supporting the impeachment of Bill Clinton. Dershowtiz concluded one recent harrangue against these millions of Americans by declaring their views "the forces of evil, evil, genuine evil." See Kenneth L. Khachigian, "Anger Fueling Left's Defense of Indefensible," *The Los Angeles Times,* Orange County Edition, January 3, 1999, p. B7. For a larger discussion of the support white liberals have offered black rage, particularly during the 1960s, see the important book by Myron Magnet, *The Dream and the Nightmare: The Sixties' Legacy to the Underclass* (New York: William Morrow, 1993).

6. This, even though black anger has at times been so acute that doctors have prescribed large doses of tranquilizers in order to calm those experiencing it. Such is the claim of black psychiatrist Alvin Poussaint in Alan Matusow, *The Unraveling of America: A History of Liberalism in the 1960s* (New York: Harper and Row, 1984), pp. 349-350. Poussaint refers to rage as exclusively caused by beatings given civil rights protestors during the civil rights movement, but Matusow points out that this anger extended well beyond unfair police practices of the 1960s, to white America as a whole decades hence. See Dinesh D'Souza, *The End of Racism* (New York: The Free Press, 1996), pp. 491-495 for a valuable discussion of black rage.

7. Ironically, despite high sensitivity to racial oppression in this country, the well-documented slavery of blacks within Africa has not attracted the concern of civil rights organizations here. See Joseph R. Gregory, "African Slavery 1996," *First Things,* May 1996, pp. 37-39, Jeff Jacoby, "Civil Rights Groups Yawn at African Slavery," *The Orange County Register,* April 4, 1996, p. Metro 9; Thomas Sowell, "Some Hidden Truths in Black History Month," *The Orange County Register,* February 18, 1997, p. Metro 9; and Sowell, "Where Is Outrage About Black-on Black Slavery?" *Human Events,* March 7, 1997, p. 14; David Aikman, "Slavery in Our Time," *The American Spectator,* February 1997, pp. 52-53. On the genocidal destruction of African life by Africans, and the lukewarm response of American civil rights groups, see Keith B. Richburg, *Out of America: A Black Man Confronts Africa* (New York: Basic Books, 1997). For a discussion of black anger and major media's role in fomenting that anger, see the insightful discussion by Dennis Prager, "The Media Distorted the Racial Divide Over the Simpson Verdicts," in *The Prager Perspective,* February 15, 1997.

8. Karen Grigsby Bates, "In the Senate, Hearing the Sounds of the Noose and Jim

Crow," *The Los Angeles Times*, January 15, 1999, p. B9.

9. D'Souza, *The End of Racism*, p. 5

10. *Ibid.*

11. *Ibid.*

12. Frederick Lynch, *The Diversity Machine* (New York: The Free Press, 1997), p. 117.

13. D'Souza, *The End of Racism*, p. 404. On February 10, 1997 a federal jury found Lemrick Nelson guilty of violating Yankel Rosenbaum's civil rights for the killing. For that offense he faces six to 20 years in prison under sentencing guidelines. See "Black Guilty in Civil-Rights Trial Over Jewish Scholar Slain in Riot," *The Orange County Register*, February 11, 1997, p. News 20.

14. Dennis Prager, "Black Candidates and White Voters," *The Prager Perspective*, December 15, 1996. p. 4.

15. Quoted in D'Souza, *The End of Racism*, p. 6. See Ellis Cose, *The Rage of a Privileged Class* (New York: HarperCollins, 1993).

16. For concise biographical information, see the Associated Press obituary, "Kwame Ture, 57, civil rights activist," *The Orange County Register*, November 16, 1998, p. Metro 4.

17. For the account of Ture's funeral, which was part memorial service, part Leftist rally, see the Associated Press story of November 22, 1998, "Father of 'Black Power' Remembered."

18. Michael Hill, Associated Press, "Brawley Advisers Found Liable," July 13, 1998. For comprehensive discussion of the Brawley case, see Robert McFadden, et al., *Outrage: The Story Behind the Tawana Brawley Hoax* (New York: Bantam Books, 1990).

19. G. J. Krupey, "Black on White Crime," David Horowitz and Peter Collier, eds., *The Race Card* (Rocklin, CA: Prima Publishing, 1997), p. 203.

20. Dennis Prager, *Happiness Is a Serious Problem* (New York: HarperCollins, 1998), p. 80. On the widespread nature of victim-centered thinking in American life today, see Charles Sykes, *A Nation of Victims* (New York: St. Martin's Press, 1992).

21. "The Week," *National Review*, August 17, 1998, p. 10.

22. Larry Neumeister, "Black Music Promoters Sue Agencies," Associated Press news report, November 21, 1998.

23. Cited in Robert L. Woodson, "The New Politics in Action," in "Left and Right: The Emergence of a New Politics in the 1990s?," a conference sponsored by the Heritage Foundation and the Progressive Foundation, Washington, DC, October 30, 1991, p. 47.

24. "Gap Grows Between Black Middle Class and Those Mired in Poverty, Study Finds," *Los Angeles Times*, August 9, 1991, p. A27.

25. Thomas Sowell, *The Economics and Politics of Race* (New York: William Morrow Co., 1983), p. 194.

26. Thomas Sowell, *Civil Rights: Rhetoric or Reality?* (New York: William Morrow Co., 1984), pp. 80-81. For a thoughtful examination of dynamics affecting average group income, and the subtleties of measuring group income statistically, see Sowell's book *The Vision of the Annointed: Self Congratulation as a Basis for Social Policy* (New York: Basic Books, 1995), pp. 31-63. For an extended analysis of the relationship between race and culture in economic, political and social contexts, see Sowell's *Race and Culture: A Worldview* (New York: Basic Books, 1994).

27. See *Time*, March 13, 1989, pp. 58-68.

28. Richard Miniter, "Why Is America's Black Middle Class Strangely Fragile?" *The American Enterprise*, November/December 1998, p. 32.

29. Karl Zinsmeister, "When Black and White Turn Gray," *The American Enterprise*,

November/December 1998, p. 5.

30. William Raspberry, "Naysayers Aside, Blacks Are Making Progress," *Los Angeles Times*, August 7, 1998, p. B9.

31. For discussion of the social and politcal implications of this profile, see David Horowitz, "Denzel, Dennis and Shaq Belie the 'Color Bar'," *Los Angeles Times*, July 23, 1996, p. B7.

32. Raspberry, "Naysayers Aside, Blacks are Making Progress."

33. Civil rights groups also evince a profound hypocrisy in their continual failure to condemn cop-killing as strongly as they condemn perceived acts of police brutality. Let a white police man kick a black man without clear and convinving cause, and civil rights groups will hold a press conference, condemn racist police brutality, and initiate expensive law suits. But let a white policeman be killed in the line of duty, and these same groups will say nothing. Nothing! This is an outrage, and a stunning hypocrisy. In neither the killings of officers Brian Brown, Steven Gajda or Filbert Cuesta (all of the LAPD), did the NAACP, the Los Angeles Urban League or Johnnie Cochran, Jr., have a press conference to condemn the anarchy, or in any public way express revulsion at those murders, murders which are nothing less than an attack on the social fabric itself. For the tragic story of Officer Brown's murder, see "Careening Sequence of Violence Claims Officer," *Los Angeles Times*, December 1, 1998, p. A1.

34. For a summary discussion of black groups' hypocrisy on this point, see Walter Williams, "A Deafening Silence," *Issues & Views*, Spring 1998, p. 1. See also note seven above.

35. "Black Teen Suicide Rate Rising Rapidly Since 80's," *Los Angeles Times*, March 20, 1998, p. A18.

36. "AIDS Among Black Women Seen as a Growing Problem," *Los Angeles Times*, July 24, 1998, p. A1.

37. "AIDS: Greater Rate of Infection Among Black Women Seen," *Los Angeles Times*, July 24, 1998, p. A22.

38. *Ibid.*

39. *Ibid.*

40. Associated Press, "NAACP to Sue Gun Industry," story by Paul Shepard, July 11, 1999.

41. Quoted in Dennis Prager, "Looking Out From the Sane Asylum," *The Prager Perspective*, June 1, 1999, p. 2. Note the bitter contempt for white conservatives this remark demonstrates.

42. Brad Stetson, "The Sage of South-Central: An Interview with Larry Elder," in Stan Faryna, Brad Stetson and Joseph G. Conti, eds., *Black and Right*, p. 162.

43. For an exception, see David Horowitz, "Identifying Black Racism: The Last Taboo," *The Orange County Register*, December 10, 1995, p. Commentary 3. For a comprehensive look at this question, see Dinesh D'Souza's chapter "Bigotry in Black and White: Can African Americans Be Racist?" in his book *The End of Racism*, pp. 387-429. See also Jared Taylor, *Paved With Good Intentions* (New York: Carrol and Graf, 1992), pp. 64-73, 233-240, 256-260.

44. On CNN's "Capital Gang" program, August 22, 1998.

45. Gregory Kane, "Racial Murders Come in All Colors in America," *Los Angeles Times*, July 15, 1998, p. B7.

46. "The Itererant Incendiary," *Newsweek*, September 14, 1998, p. 32.

47 Quoted in D'Souza, *The End of Racism*, p. 401

48 "The Itererant Incendiary," p. 32.

49. D'Souza, *The End of Racism*, p. 406

50. Jim Sleeper, *Liberal Racism* (New York: Viking, 1997), p. 126.

51. *Ibid.*

52. Camille. O. Cosby, "Camille Cosby: America taught my son's killer to hate blacks," *USA Today*, July 8, 1998, p. 15A.

53. Cal Thomas, "Clinton's Race Panel: Lies in Black and White," *Human Events*, October 16, 1998, p. 18.

54. "Blacks See Familiar Persecution in Clinto Plight," *Los Angeles Times*, September 14, 1998, p. A21.

55. D'Souza, *The End of Racism*, p. 400.

56. *Ibid.*, p. 403.

57. Quoted in Ibid.

58. Stephen Thernstrom and Abigail Thernstrom, *America in Black and White* (New York: Simon & Schuster, 1997, p. 514.

59. Krupey, "Black on White Crime," p. 201.

60. *Ibid.*, p. 197.

61. *Ibid.*, p. 197.

62. Mona Charen, "Honesty a great challenge in race relations," *The Orange County Register*, March 2, 1999, p. Metro 7.

63. Krupey, "Black on White Crime," p. 198.

64. *Ibid.*

65. Cal Thomas, "Clinton's Race Panel: Lies in Black and White," *Human Events*, October 16, 1998, p. 18.

66. Walter Williams, "Blacks can solve their problems if they will," *The Orange County Register*, July 20, 1998, p. Metro 7.

67. Ward Connerly, "Back to Equality, *Imprimis*, February 1998, p. 3.

68. Shelby Steele, *A Dream Deferred* (New York: HarperCollins, 1998), p. 185.

69. Dinesh D'Souza, "A World Without Racial Preferences," *The Weekly Standard*, November 30/December 7, 1998, p. 41.

Chapter Three: The Problem with Men and Women

1. William J. Bennett, *The Index of Leading Cultural Indicators* (New York: Simon and Schuster, 1994), pp. 58, 47, 78.

2. David Blankenhorn, *Fatherless America* (New York: Basic Books, 1995), p. 1.

3. Barbara Whithead, "Dan Quayle Was Right," *The Atlantic Monthly*, April 1993. See also the excellent articles on the topic of fatherhood in the special issue of *The American Enterprise*, September/October 1999, pp. 24-53

4. Maggie Gallagher, "Fatherless Boys Grow up into Dangerous Men," *The Wall Street Journal*, December 1, 1998, p. A22. Of course, it is also critical that the father be a decent man, and that his interaction with his wife be civil. Fathers and mothers at war with one another cause their children to fall away from innocence. The children lose that beautiful sense of innocence and wonder at life with which they were born. They also lose the natural respect for their fathers, because they sense he's not being the example to them that he should be. And the children become resentful toward the mother, because of her anger at the father, who is not the man she knows he should be. She then turns the

kids further away from the father by means of her resentment. This destructive cycle can move from generation and generation, leaving a tremendous wake of destruction. When the father is not a proper man in the home, modeling for his children what it means to get along with other people, his children suffer greatly.

5. *Ibid.*

6. Robert H. Bork, *Slouching Towards Gomorrah* (New York: HarperCollins, 1996), p. 204. Especially valuable critiques of contemporary feminism include Danielle Crittenden, *What Our Mothers Didn't Tell Us: Why Happiness Eludes the Modern Woman* (New York: Simon & Schuster, 1999); Carolyn Graglia, *Domestic Tranquility: A Brief Against Feminsim* (Dallas: Spence Publishing, 1998); Wendy Shalit, *A Return to Modesty* (New York: The Free Press, 19999); Christina Hoff Sommers, *Who Stole Feminism?* (New York: Simon & Schuster, 1994); Cathy Young, *Ceasefire!: Why Women and Men Must Join Forces to Achieve True Equality* (New York: The Free Press, 1999).

7. John A. Barnes, "The Boyfriend Problem," *The Weekly Standard*, December 14, 1998, p. 22.

8. *Ibid.*, p. 23.

9. *Ibid.*, p. 22.

10. For a fine analysis of popular moral relativism, see Francis J. Beckwith and Gregory Koukl, *Relativism: Feet Firmly Planted in Mid-Air* (Grand Rapids: Baker Book House, 1998).

11. "Sharon Stone Says Keep Condoms Near," Associated Press, December 2, 1998.

Chapter Four: The Problem with Abortion

1. Valuable pro-life books which make this case are Randy Alcorn, *Pro-Life Answers to Pro-Choice Arguments* (Sisters, OR: Questar Publishers, 1992); Francis J. Beckwith, *Politically Correct Death: Answering the Arguments for Abortion Rights* (Grand Rapids, MI: Baker Books, 1991); James Burtchaell, *Rachel Weeping* (San Francisco: Harper & Row, 1982); Patrick Lee, *Abortion and Unborn Human Life* (Washington, DC: Catholic University Press, 1996); and Brad Stetson, Ed., *The Silent Subject: Reflections on the Unborn in American Culture* (Westport, CT: Praeger Publishers, 1996). Some of the material in this chapter draws from Stetson, *The Silent Subject*, pp. 1-15 and Brad Stetson, *Human Dignity and Contemporary Liberalism* (Westport, CT: Praeger Publishers, 1998), pp. 130-146.

2. *Witchita Eagle*, October 7, 1977. For a full discussion of Tiller and his abortion business, see Gregg L. Cunningham, "Wave of the Future?" *National Review*, November 10, 1997, pp. 36-38.

3. These facts are documented in Jessica Shaver's article, "Attack on Doctor Shifts Focus from the Violence of Abortion," *Orange County Register*, 29 August 1993, Commentary p. 3. Regarding the ethical issues surrounding violent attacks on doctors who perform abortions—attacks which have rightly been condemned by virtually all opponents of abortion—see Richard John Neuhaus, "Bloody-Minded Compassion," *First Things*, No. 40, February 1994, pp. 48-50; and "Killing Abortionists: A Symposium," *First Things*, No. 48, December 1994, pp. 24-31.

4. *WORLD*, September 5, 1998, p. 13.

5. Mona Charen, "Feelings, not morality, now constitute law," *The Orange County Register*, July 16, 1998, p. Metro 9.

6. "Attempted homicide alleged in fetal intoxication case," *USA Today*, September 6, 1996, p. 8A.

7. "Woman Who Shot Herself Is Charged in Fetus' Death," *Los Angeles Times*, September 10, 1994, p. A34.

8. "Fetus to Get Surgery for Birth Defect," *Santa Barbara News Press*, September 9, 1993, p. A1.

9. Meki Cox, "Baby Kicking After Open-Womb Surgery," Associated Press, July 4, 1998. For discussion of similar cases of fetal surgery, see "Birth successful after surgery in the womb," *The Orange County Register*, October 29, 1998, p. News 12; and "New approach for twins with a missing heart," *The Orange County Register*, October 29, 1998, p. News 13.

10. "Driver sentenced to 16 years in death of premature baby," *The Orange County Register*, October 22, 1996, p. News 17.

11. Susan Carpenter McMillan, "...While in California, a Court Affirms the Humanity of a Fetus," *Los Angeles Times*, May 20, 1994, p. B11.

12. "Murder Charge Is Rejected in Drug-Related Stillbirth," *Los Angeles Times*, August 22, 1992, p. A13.

13. See "Pregnancy negligence not prosecuted," *The Orange County Register*, Aug. 11, 1996, p. Metro 7. For an excellent examination of the current configuration of legal protections for the unborn and fetal homicide laws, see the cover story, "Rights of the Unborn," *USA Today*, December 12, 1996.

14. "Beating the mother of unborn child not a felony, court rules," *The Orange County Register*, March 17, 1998.

15. These developmental markers are noted in standard texts, including F. Beck, D. B. Moffat, and D. P. Davies, *Human Embryology* , 2nd ed. (Oxford: Blackwell, 1985); Keith L. Moore, *The Developing Human: Clinically Oriented Embryology*, 2nd ed. (Philadelphia: W. B. Saunders, 1977); Andre E. Hellegers, "Fetal Development," in Thomas A. Mappes and Jane S. Zembaty, eds., *Biomedical Ethics* (New York: Macmillan 1981), pp. 405-409; Landrum Shettles and David Rorvik, *Rites of Life: The Scientific Evidence of Life Before Birth* (Grand Rapids: Zondervan Publishing, 1983).

16. Sidney Callahan, "The First Stage of Life *Is* Life," *Los Angeles Times*, June 19 1991, p. B7. Of course one common way some commentators attempt to avoid Callahan's conclusions is by importing gradations of human life into consideration of the "ontological" status of the unborn. But any and all talk of "partial human-ness" is inevitably arbitrary and subjective, since it must appeal to a particular religious or otherwise ideological touchstone of "complete human-ness," the warrant for which is itself going to be private and parochial—and in strong need of comprehensive justification. Some writers who appeal to gradations of humanity often reserve "partial human-ness" for the earliest stages of pregnancy (e.g., one day, three weeks), where they presumably see abortion as unproblematic. It is important to point out, however, that the earliest abortions are not performed before six weeks postconception, so that the doctor performing the procedure is able to reassemble ex utero the dismembered body, in order to verify the completion of the procedure, and reduce the risk of infection. Thus, the appeal to embryonic "partial human-ness"—even if wrongly accepted as legitimate—is irrelevant to the abortion debate, since no abortions are performed at that stage of pregnancy. The specter of RU-486, the so-called "abortion pill," being employed as an abortifacient at this early stage of pregnancy is problematic as well, since (1) it is still a means of abortion and susceptible to all the arguments against abortion; and (2) it is simply untrue that RU-486 is safe and

clinically unproblematic. For two brief discussions of some of the dangers of RU-486, see Janice G. Raymond, "RU-486: Miracle Drug Turns Nasty," *Los Angeles Times*, April 11, 1993, p. M5 and Callahan, "The First Stage of Life *Is* Life."

17. George Flesh, "Why I No Longer Do Abortions," *Los Angeles Times*, September 12, 1991. I should point out that Dr. Flesh was not prevented from terminating Jeffrey's "potential life," as he says, but Jeffrey's *actual* life, along with the future realization of Jeffrey's potential.

It is instructive to note that Dr. Flesh's experience underlines the plain yet often overlooked biological and linguistic reality that words like "embryo" and "fetus" have *developmental* not *ontological* significance. That is, they refer to a definite and established type of being *at a certain stage of its existence*, not a being which at its present stage is ontologically different from what it will later become.

18. All four remarks drawn from Mark Collette, "Pang of Conscience," *WORLD*, January 17, 1998.

19. Quoted in Patrick Buchanan, "Christians, Nazis and Jesse Jackson," *Los Angeles Times*, December 13, 1994, p. B7.

20. Michael Bauman, "The Euphemisms of Abortion Hide the Crime," *Orange County Register*, January 9, 1989, reprinted in Francis J. Beckwith, *Politically Correct Death: Answering the Arguments for Abortion Rights* (Grand Rapids: Baker Book House, 1993), p. 181.

21. James Davison Hunter, *Before the Shooting Begins: Searching for Democracy in America's Culture Wars* (New York: Free Press, 1994), p. 163.

22. Some recent polls documenting this are to be found in *The Boston Globe*, March 31, 1989, pp. 1, 12; "Poll: Abortion Key for Voters," *USA Today*, January 2, 1990, pp. 1A, 2A; "Abortion Legislation Poll," *Newsweek*, July 17, 1991, p. 17; and "Gallup Poll: America is Pro-Life," *The Washington Times*, February 28, 1991, p. 1. For a clear and concise description of the current scope of abortion law, including the often denied fact that abortion in the United States is legal throughout the nine months of pregnancy, see Hunter, *Before the Shooting Begins*, pp. 247-249.

23. This is the latest annual total. See "Abortion Providers at Lowest Mark Since '73," *Los Angeles Times*, December 11, 1998, p. A45.

24. As many writers have argued, *Roe v. Wade* and the common practice of abortion benefits men not women, by freeing them from the consequences of their sexual behavior. Indeed, a significant percentage of women who abort report that they did so under pressure from a man. For discussion of males pressuring females to abort and the various psychological sequelae suffered by women as a result of abortion, see the comprehensive survey work of David C. Reardon, *Aborted Women, Silent No More* (Chicago: Loyola University Press, 1987), especially pp. 27-40; 45-47; 328-337. Of course this is a great and tragic paradox, since it is women's rights groups who championed the legalization of abortion, who defend it today with little regard for the harm it causes women, and who hold it out as *the precondition* for women's social and economic equality with men. For a sensitive statement on how and why the interests of women should not be seen as mutually exclusive with a pro-life ethic, see "A New American Compact: Caring about Women, Caring for the Unborn," *First Things*, No. 27, November 1992, pp. 43-46; and Frederica Mathewes-Green, *Real Choices: Offering Practical, Life-Affirming Alternatives to Abortion* (Sisters, OR: Questar Publications, 1994).

25. See chapter 4, "The Anatomy of Ambivalence," in Hunter, *Before the Shooting Begins*, particularly pp. 86-99, for a detailed discussion of the many nuances of public

opinion on abortion.

26. "Polls: Shift in support for abortion," *USA Today*, January 21, 1998, p. 1A. See also Linda Chavez, "GOP's position on abortion gains strength," *The Orange County Register*, January 26, 1998, p. Metro 7.

27. Nat Hentoff, "No Limit on 'Choice?' Here's the Ugly Result," *Los Angeles Times*, July 26, 1993.

28. See *National Right to Life News*, September 7, 1994, p. 20.

29. See "Abortion Deaths Cost Doctor License," *Los Angeles Times*, May 25, 1995, pp. A3, A40.

30. "ACLU Protests Release of Fetuses for Burial," *The Los Angeles Times*, October 10, 1998, p. A30.

31. Anne McFadden, "The Link Between Abortion and Child Abuse," *Family Resource Center News*, January , 1998, p. 19.

32. Bill Brown, "A Culture of Death," *WORLD*, October 10, 1998, p. 33.

33. "In the Name of the Children," *Los Angeles Times Magazine*, August 7, 1994, p. 14.

34. Sheila Chung, Letter to the Editor, *Los Angeles Times*, January 29, 1998, p. B8. See also Sydna Masse, "'Choice' Killed a Part of My Heart," *Los Angeles Times*, January 23, 1998, p. B9.

35. Nancyjo Mann, foreword to Reardon, *Aborted Women: Silent No More*, p. xvi.

36. "Abortions in America," *U. S. News & World Report*, January 19, 1998, p. 29.

37. Stephen Chapman, "Both sexes want limits on abortion," *The Orange County Register*, January 20, 1998, p. Metro 9.

38. For the complete story on Steir, and the sad tale of Sharon Hamptlon's death at his hands, see "Abortion Issue's *Cause Celebre*," *Los Angeles Times*, December 1, 1998, p. A1.

39. Paul Davenport, The Associated Press, "Doctor Suspended in Abortion Case," July 21, 1998. For more on this case, see the editorial by David Tell in *The Weekly Standard*, July 27, 1998.

40. Frederica Mathewes Green, "Beyond 'It's a Baby.'" *National Review*, December 31, 1997, p. 41.

41. "Mom the Murderer," *The Wall Street Journal*, January 2, 1998, p. A8. On this case, see also "Mothers and Killers," *Time*, July 20, 1998, p. 28, and Tucker Carlson, "Horror in the Court," *The Weekly Standard*, January 26, 1998, pp. 14-18.

42. Peter Kirsanow, "A Black Conservative Looks at Abortion," in Stan Faryna, Brad Stetson and Joseph G. Conti, eds., *Black and Right: The Bold New Voice of Black Conservatives in America* (Westport, CT: Praeger Publishers, 1997), p. 116.

43. Margaret Sanger, *Birth Control Review*, April 1933, quoted in Randy Alcorn, *Pro-Life Answers to Pro-Choice Arguments* (Sisters, OR: Multnomah Books, 1992), p. 115.

44. *Ibid.*

45. Margaret Sanger, *Pivot of Civilization* (New York: Bentano's, 1922), p. 176, quoted in Alcorn, *Pro-Life Answers to Pro-Choice Arguments*, p. 115.

46. "Abortion altered America's future," *USA Today*, January 21, 1998, p 15A.

47. "Abortion by the Numbers," *The Village Voice*, January 27, 1998.

48. On the black/white abortion rate, see the statistics from the Alan Guttmacher Institute, cited in Tom Bethell, "Roe's Disparate Impact," *The American Spectator*, June 1996, pp. 18-19. On the racist nature of some support for abortion, see "Buckley: Abortion backed by some with racist intent," *The Orange County Register*, June 2, 1996, p. News 13. See also Robert Marshall and Charles Donovan, *Blessed Are the Barren: The Social Policy of Planned Parenthood* (San Francisco: Ignatius Press, 1991) and Donald T.

Critchlow, *Intended Consequences: Birth Control, Abortion, and the Federal Government in Modern America* (New York: Oxford University Press, 1999).

49. Alan Keyes, in a speech given to the New Hampshire Republican State Committee, February 19, 1995.

50. "M. D. accused of causing girlfriend to miscarry," *The Orange County Register*, September 3, 1998, p. News 16.

51. George Weigel, "Women Reap the Rewards of Roe in Abuse," *Los Angeles Times*, November 29, 1992, p. M5. See also Wendy Shalit, "Whose Choice?" *National Review*, May 18, 1998, pp. 28-30.

52. Frederica Mathewes-Green, "The Tell-Tale Heart," *Family Resources Center News*, August 1998, page 11.

53. "Abortions in America," *U. S. News & World Report*, January 19, 1998, p. 25.

54. For detailed statements from women who have aborted, and for analysis of the psycho-emotional sequelae often experienced by them, see Reardon, *Aborted Women: Silent No More*.

55. For comprehensive analysis see David Blankenhorn, *Fatherless America: Confronting Our Most Urgent Social Problem* (New York: Basic Books, 1995) and David Popenoe, *Life Without Father* (New York: Martin Kessler Books, 1996).

56. Blankenhorn, *Fatherless America: Confronting Our Most Urgent Social Problem*, p. 1.

57. See the discussion on this general point by Warren Farrell, *The Myth of Male Power* (New York: Berkley Books, 1993), p. 13.

58. James Q Wilson traces a similar thought pattern in his *The Moral Sense* (New York: The Free Press, 1993), p. 175.

59. "Man Sues Mate For Becoming Pregnant Against His Will," *Los Angeles Times*, November 23, 1998, p. A12.

Chapter Five: The Problem with Immigration

1. California's new Democratic governor, Gray Davis, was only too pleased to see the will of the people thwarted by the courts, promising visiting Mexican president Ernesto Zedillo that he would do everything he could to prevent the measure from becoming law. As Zedillo confidently told a large group of Mexicans living in Southern California, "I have received the commitment of the governor to do whatever he can so the negative effects that this Proposition 187 could generate...do not materialize." "Zedillo Courts LA's Latino Community," *Los Angeles Times*, May 22, 1999, p. A3. The Mexican president was later congratulated by a high-ranking Hispanic politician in California, Assembly Speaker Antonio Villaraigosa, for having a "great impact in defeating Proposition 187." See Frank Del Olmo, "Assembly Speaker Cut Off a Rung on His Political Ladder," *The Los Angeles Times*, August 9, 1999, p. B9. The political perversity of this remark is hard to comprehend: a leading California lawmaker thanks the president of another country for helping ensure that a bill voted into law by a clear majority of California citizens never actually takes effect.

2. Roberto Rivera, "Will El Norte Change or Be Changed?" *Books & Culture*, July/August 1999, p. 6. Most official estimates place the number of illegal immigrants living in California at a minimum of 2 million.

3. "High School District Mulls Suing Mexico," *Los Angeles Times*, May 28, 1999, p. B11. Martin has also called for the Anaheim school district to sue Mexico for the estimated 10 million dollar annual cost of educating illegal immigrants from that coun-

try in Anaheim's public schools.

4. See "INS running out of cells for illegal-immigrant criminals," *The Orange County Register*, February 26, 1999, p. News 34, and "INS jail deportation program in Anaheim hailed as a success," *The Orange County Register*, May 13, 1999, p. News 11.

5. The dearth of public discussion of Hispanic ethnocentrism and even racism is a remarkable phenomenon. Race consciousness among Hispanics is as intense as among many black Afrocentrists, and, as with blacks, it sometimes generates anti-white violence. The most notable example recently in Southern California was the beating of a white elementary school principal by two Hispanic men who said, during the assault, "We don't want you here anymore...do you understand, white principal?" The principal was known to support English only instruction in school, which had just become law with the passage of Proposition 227. See "Beating of principal exposes culture clash," *The Orange County Register*, February 16, 1999, p. Metro 4. Of course the extent of racially motivated violence by Latinos is hard to gauge since the federal government inexplicably counts them as a category of victim on the federal government's hate-crime incident report form, but not as a category of perpetrator. For perpetrators only, they are subsumed under the category "White."

6. See "How Santa Ana won the prize," *The Orange County Register*, January 14, 1999, p. News 10.

7. See "Santa Ana Unified schools to get nearly 600,000 in federal funds," *The Orange County Register*, April 29, 1999, P. Metro 5.

8. See, for example, John J. Miller, *The Unmaking of Americans* (New York: The Free Press, 1998), pp. 3-4. For explanation of why Mexicans living in southern California, more than other Hispanics there, retain nationalist feelings and are disinclined to assimilate into the American identity, see Peter Brimelow, *Alien Nation* (New York: HarperCollins, 1996), pp. 272-273.

9. "Mexico Rejects Voting Abroad Plan," Adolfo Garcia, AP newswire, July 1, 1999. Further showing the commitment many Mexicans living in the United States have to remaining Mexicans is the fact that they have the lowest naturalization rate of any immigration population. See Linda Chavez, "Hispanics Must Emphasize Naturalization," *The Orange County Register*, October 20, 1999, p. Local News 9.

10. *Ibid.* Indeed, the Mexican state of Michoacan receives more than six million dollars each year from Mexican immigrants living in the U. S., an amount equal to that state's budget for the year 1996. See "Making a Difference," *The Orange County Register*, September 2, 1999, p. Accent 6.

11. "Win: 'This street is Mexico,'" *The Orange County Register*, June 14, 1998, p. Metro 6.

12. Lawrence Harrison, "The Cultural Roots of Poverty," *The Wall Street Journal*, July 13, 1999, p. A22. On the critical role of cultural values in any population's social and economic progress, see Harrison's important study, *Who Prospers? How Cultural Values Shape Economic and Political Success* (New York: Basic Books, 1992). For further discussion of how current immigration patterns harm America's poor, see George J. Borjas, *Heaven's Door* (Princeton, NJ: Princeton University Press, 1999).

Chapter Six: The Problem with Education

1. William J. Bennett, *The Index of Leading Cultural Indicators* (New York: Simon & Schuster, 1994), p.82.

2. William J. Bennet and Chester E. Finn, Jr., "Idea Whose Time Has Come: 'Straight As,'" *Los Angeles Times,* June 23, 1999, p. B9.

3. *Ibid.,* p. 83.

4. Walter E. Williams, *Do the Right Thing* (Stanford: Hoover Institution Press, 1995), p. 93.

5. Mathew Miller, "Board Game," *The New Republic,* April 26 and May 3, 1999, p. 18.

6. Walter E. Williams, *Do the Right Thing* (Stanford: Hoover Institution Press, 1995), p. 95.

7. "Support for vouchers high among blacks and Hispanics," *The Orange County Register,* December 27, 1997, p. News 1.

8. William Tucker, "The Choices Are Expanding," *The American Spectator,* September 1998, p. 30.

9. Andrew Young, "Let Parents Choose Their Kids' Schools," *Los Angeles Times,* April 29, 1999, p. B11.

10. See "Smaller Schools Called Antidote to Alienation," *Los Angeles Times,* May 19, 1999, p. A1.

11. See "Private Schools Succeed with Holistic Approaches," *Los Angeles Times,* June 16, 1999, p. B2.

12. For discussion of the fairness of vouchers, see John Coons, "School Choice as Simple Justice, *First Things,* April 1992, pp. 15-28.

13. Walter E. Williams, *Do the Right Thing* (Stanford: Hoover Institution Press, 1995), p. 91.

14. Teacher's unions, of course, are the strongest opponents of vouchers. In 1993, the California Teachers Association, the politically correct but monstrously powerful public schoolteachers' union, spent 13 million dollars to defeat a voucher ballot initiative. They outspent supporters of the initiative by a stunning 4 to 1 ratio (See "Vouchers," *The Orange County Register,* May 3, 1999, p. News 6). Clearly they are afraid of competition.

15. Matthew Miller, "A Bold Experiment to Fix City Schools," *The Atlantic Monthly,* July 1999, p. 16. In this article Miller makes the point that there is also a long history of liberal or "progressive" support for vouchers, a point totally unrecognized by contemporary liberal lobbies like the NEA, ACLU and, of course, the NAACP.

16. Robert L. Woodson, Jr., *The Triumphs of Joseph: How Today's Community Healers Are Reviving Our Streets and Neighborhoods* (New York: The Free Press, 1998), p. 19.

17. Walter E. Williams, "What American Education Needs," *The Freeman,* April 1999, p. 64.

18. Mark Gerson, *In the Classroom* (New York: The Free Press, 1997). p. 24.

19. For descriptive discussions of the charge "acting white" and what it means to black kids, see John Ogbu and Signithia Fordham, "Black Students' School Success: Coping with the Burden of 'Acting White'," *Urban Review* 18, no. 3, pp. 176-206; "The Hidden Hurdle," *Time,* March 16, 1992, p. 44; "Racial gap among well-to-do baffles school officials," *The Orange County Register,* July 4, 1999; "Acting White," ABC News 20/20, June 7, 1999 air date.

20. If it surprises you to hear this, you either don't live in a black community or you don't pay attention to black popular culture.

21. Despite the prevalence of this addled way of behaving in many inner-city black schools, the fact is that there is a rich tradition in American black life of private neighbor-

hood academies and private schools which are among the highest achieving schools in the country, and routinely create students who absolutely excel in academics. Needless to say, the epithet "acting white" is not present at such institutions. For discussion of some of these outstanding black private schools, like Harambee Preparatory School, the Marcus Garvey School, see Stephen E. Berk, *A Time to Heal: John Perkins, Community Development, and Racial Reconciliation* (Grand Rapids, MI: Baker Books, 1997), pp. 384-391 and Williams, *Do the Right Thing*, pp. 86-87, respectively.

22. "20/20," Charles Gibson reporting, June 7, 1999 broadcast.

23. Armstrong Williams, "Vouchers Give Chance at Best Education," *Los Angeles Times*, April 22, 1999, p. B9.

Chapter Seven: What Americans Should Do Now

1. "College Deletes Marriage Boast," Associated Press, December 8, 1998.

2. Bennett, *The Index of Leading Cultural Indicators*, p. 47.

3. *Ibid.*

4. *Ibid.*, p. 48.

5. *Ibid.*, p. 50.

6. *Ibid.*, p. 58.

7. *Ibid.*, p. 59

8. *Ibid.*

9. Keith Richburg, *Out of America* (New York: Basic Books, 1997), p. 165.

10. For helpful discussions debunking the claims Afrocentrists make regarding the glory of Africa, see John J. Miller, ed., *Alternatives to Afrocentrism* (Washington, DC, Center for the New American Community, Manhattan Institute, 1994), and Mary Lefkowitz, *Not Out of Africa: How Afrocentrism Became an Excuse to Teach Myth* (New York: Basic Books, 1996).

11. Richburg, *Out of America*, p. 227.

12. Brilliant discussion of what such submission might mean, and how it could be accomplished, is found in philosopher Dallas Willard's book, *The Divine Conspiracy* (New York: HarperSanFrancisco, 1998).

Recommended Reading

Chapter 1: My Story

Carson, Ben with Cecil Murphey, *Gifted Hands*. New York: HarperCollins, 1993.

Connerly, Ward. *Creating Equal: My Fight Against Race Preferences*. San Francisco: Encounter Books, 2000.

Darden, Christopher, with Jess Walter. *In Contempt*. New York: HarperCollins, 1996.

Early, Gerald, ed., *Lure and Loathing: Essays on Race, Identity and the Ambivalence of Assimilation*. New York: Penguin, 1993.

Foster, Ezola. *What's Right for All Americans!* with a foreword by Walter E. Williams. Waco, TX: WRS Publishing, 1995.

Franks, Gary. *Searching for the Promised Land*. New York: HarperCollins, 1996.

Gilder, George. *Visible Man*. San Francisco: ICS Press, re-issued version, 1995.

Hamblin, Ken. *Pick a Better Country: An Unassuming Colored Guy Speaks His Mind About America*. New York: Simon & Schuster, 1996.

Horowitz, David. *Radical Son*. New York: The Free Press, 1997.

Keyes, Alan. *Masters of the Dream: The Strength and Betrayal of Black America*. New York: William Morrow, 1995.

Loury, Glenn. *One by One From the Inside Out: Essays and Reviews on Race and Responsibility in America*. New York: The Free Press, 1995.

Powell, Colin with Jospeh Persico. *My American Journey*. New York: Random House, 1995.

Prager, Dennis. *Happiness Is a Serious Problem*. New York: HarperCollins, 1998.

Schuyler, George S. *Black and Conservative: The Autobiography of George S. Schuyler*, New Rochelle: Arlington House Publishers, 1966.

Suskind, Ron. *A Hope in the Unseen*. New York: Broadway Books, 1998.

Williams, Armstrong. *Beyond Blame: How We Can Succeed by Breaking the Dependency Barrier*. New York: The Free Press, 1995.

Witt, Edwin T. *Witt's End: Fulfilling the American Dream*. Victorville, CA: E & C Publishers, 1996.

Chapter 2: The Problem with Race

Bennett, William J., John J. DiIulio, Jr. and John P. Walters, *Body Count*. New York: Simon & Schuster, 1996.

Blankenhorn, David. *Fatherless America: Confronting Our Most Urgent Social Problem*. New York: Basic Books, 1995.

Conti, Joseph G. and Brad Stetson. *Challenging the Civil Rights Establishment: Profiles of a New Black Vanguard*. Westport, CT: Praeger Publishers, 1993.

Collier, Peter and David Horowitz, eds. *Second Thoughts About Race in America*. Lanham, MD: Madison Books, *1991.*

————, eds. *The Race Card*. Rocklin, CA: Prima Publishing.

Crouch, Stanley. *The All-American Skin Game*. New York: Random House, 1995.

D'Souza, Dinesh. *The End of Racism*. New York: The Free Press, 1995.

Faryna, Stan, Brad Stetson and Joseph G. Conti, eds., *Black and Right: The Bold New Voice of Black Conservatives in America*. Westport, CT: Praeger Publishers, 1997.

Horowitz, David. *Hating Whitey: And Other Progressive Causes.* Dallas, TX: Spence Publishing, 1999.

Magnet, Myron. *The Dream and the Nightmare.* New York: William Morrow, 1993.

Richburg, Keith B. *Out of America.* New York: Basic Books, 1997.

Sleeper, Jim. *The Closest of Strangers.* New York: W.W. Norton and Company, 1990.

———. *Liberal Racism.* New York: Viking, 1997.

Smith, Errol. *37 Things Every Black Man Needs to Know.* Valencia, CA: St. Clair Rene Publishing, 1991.

———. *37 More Things Every Black Man and Woman Needs to Know.* Valencia, CA: St. Clair Rene Publishing, 1994

Sniderman, Paul M. and Thomas Piazza. *The Scar of Race.* Cambridge, MA: Harvard University Press, 1993.

Sowell, Thomas. *The Economics and Politics of Race.* New York: William Morrow, 1983.

Steele, Shelby. *The Content of Our Character.* New York, St. Martin's Press, 1990.

———. *A Dream Deferred.* New York: HarperCollins, 1998.

Thernstrom, Stephen & Abigail. *America in Black and White.* New York: Simon & Schuster, 1997.

Thomas, Clarence. *Confronting the Future.* Washington, DC: Regnery Gateway, 1992

Williams, Walter. *Do the Right Thing.* Stanford, CA: Hoover Institution Press, 1995.

Woodson, Robert L. *A Summons to Life.* Cambridge, MA: Ballinger Publishing, 1981.

Wortham, Anne. *The Other Side of Racism.* Columbus: Ohio State University Press, 1981.

Chapter 3: The Problem with Men and Women

Bork, Robert H. *Slouching Towards Gomorrah.* New York: HarperCollins, 1996.

Cheney, Lynn V. *Telling the Truth.* New York: Simon & Schuster, 1995.

Crittenden, Danielle. *What Our Mothers Didn't Tell Us: Why Happiness Eludes the Modern Woman.* New York: Simon & Schuster, 1999.

Graglia, Carolyn. *Domestic Tranquility: A Brief Against Feminism.* Dallas: Spence Publishing, 1998.

Gray, John. *Men Are from Mars, Women Are from Venus.* New York: HarperCollins, 1992.

Hunter, James Davison. *Culture Wars: The Struggle to Define America.* Basic Books, 1991.

McCallum, Dennis, Ed. *The Death of Truth: What's Wrong with Multiculturalism, The Rejection of Reason and the New Postmodern Diversity.* Minneapolis: Bethany House, 1996.

Paglia, Camille. *Sexual Pernonae.* New York: Vintage, 1991.

Patai, Daphne and Noretta Koertge. *Professing Feminism: Cautionary Tales from the Strange World of Women's Studies.* New York: Basic Books, 1994.

Patterson, Orlando. *Rituals of Blood: Consequences of Slavery in Two Centuries.* Washington, DC: Counterpoint Press, 1999

Popenoe, David. *Life Without Father.* New York: Martin Kessler Books, 1996.

Reeves, Thomas. *The Empty Church.* New York: The Free Press, 1996.

Shalit, Wendy. *A Return to Modesty.* New York: The Free Press, 1999.

Sommers, Christina Hoff, *Who Stole Feminism?* New York: Simon & Schuster, 1994.

Stein, Benjamin J. *Tommy & Me.* New York: The Free Press, 1998.

Stetson, Brad. *Human Dignity and Contemporary Liberalism.* Westport, CT: Praeger Publishers, 1998.

Wetzel, Richard, *Sexual Wisdom.* Ann Arbor, MI: Proctor Publications, 1998.

Chapter 4: The Problem with Abortion

Alcorn, Randy. *Pro-Life Answers to Pro-Choice Arguments.* Sisters, OR.: Multnomah Books, 1992.

Andrusko, Dave, ed. *To Rescue the Future.* Toronto and Harrison, NY: Life Cycle Books, 1983.

Ankerberg, John, and John Weldon. *When Does Life Begin?* Brentwood, TN: Wolgemuth and Hyatt, 1989.

Beckwith, Francis J. *Politically-Correct Death: Answering the Arguments for Abortion Rights.* Grand Rapids: Baker Book House, 1993.

Belz, Mark. *Suffer the Little Children.* Westchester, IL: Crossway Books, 1989.

Brown, Harold O.J. *Death Before Birth.* Nashville, TN: Thomas Nelson, 1977.

Brown, Judy, and Paul Brown. *Choices in Matters of Life and Death.* Avon, NJ: Magnificat Press, 1987.

Burtchaell, James Tunstead. *Rachel Weeping: The Case Against Abortion.* San Francisco: Harper & Row, 1982.

Christian, Scott Rickly. *The Woodland Hills Tragedy.* Westchester, IL: Crossway Books, 1985.

Cochrane, Linda. *Women in Rama: A Postabortion Bible Study.* Falls Church, VA: Christian Action Council, 1987.

Critchelow, Donald T. *Intended Consequences: Birth Control, Abortion, and the Federal Government in Modern America.* New York: Oxford University Press, 1999.

Everett, Carol. *The Scarlet Lady: Confessions of a Successful Abortionist.* Brentwood, TN: Wolgemuth and Hyatt, 1991.

Fowler, Paul. *Abortion: Toward and Evangelical Consensus.* Portland, OR: Multnomah Books, 1987.

Frasier, Debra. *On the Day You Were Born.* San Diego: Harcourt Brace, 1991.

Garton, Jean. *Who Broke the Baby?* Minneapolis: Bethany House, 1979.

Grant, George. *Grand Illusions: The Legacy of Planned Parenthood.* Brentwood, TN: Wolgemuth and Hyatt, 1988.

Hensley, Jeff Lane, ed. *The Zero People.* Ann Arbor: Servant Books, 1983.

Hinze, Sarah. *Life Before Birth.* Springville, UT: Cedar Fort, 1993.

Hunter, James Davison. *Before the Shooting Begins: Searching for Democracy in America's Culture Wars.* New York: Free Press, 1994.

Kennedy, D. James. *Abortion: Cry of Reality.* Fort Lauderdale, FL: Coral Ridge Ministries, 1989.

Koerbel, Pam. *Abortion's Second Victim.* Wheaton, IL: Victor Books, 1986.

Kolata, Gina. *The Baby Doctors: Probing the Limits of Fetal Medicine.* New York: Dell Publishing, 1990.

Koop, C. Everett, and Francis A. Schaeffer. *Whatever Happened to the Human Race?* Wheaton, IL: Tyndale House, 1976.

Koop, C. Everett. *The Right to Live: The Right to Die.* Old Tappan, NJ: Revell, 1979.

Marshall, Robert, and Charles Donovan. *Blessed Are the Barren: The Social Policy of Planned Parenthood.* San Francisco: Ignatius Press, 1991.

Mathewes-Green, Frederica. *Real Choices: Offering Practical, Life-Affirming Alternatives to Abortion.* Sisters, OR: Questar Publications, 1994.

Michels, Nancy. *Helping Women Recover from Abortion.* Minneapolis: Bethany House, 1988.

Moreland, J. P., and Norman L. Geisler. *The Life and Death Debate: Moral Issues of Our Time.* Westport, CT: Praeger Publishers, 1990.

Reardon, David C. *Aborted Women, Silent No More.* Chicago: Loyola University Press, 1987.

Reisser, Teri and Paul. *Help for the Post-Abortion Woman.* Grand Rapids: Zondervan Publishing House, 1989.
Saltenberger, Ann. *Every Woman Has a Right to Know the Dangers of Legal Abortion.* Glassboro, NJ: Air-Plus Enterprises, 1983.
Sanger, Margaret. *Woman and the New Race.* New York: Truth Publishing, 1920.
Selby, Terry. *The Mourning After.* Grand Rapids: Baker Book House, 1990.
Shettles, Landrum and David Rorvik. *Rites of Life: The Scientific Evidence for Life Before Birth.* Grand Rapids: Zondervan Publishing House, 1983.
Stetson, Brad, Ed. *The Silent Subject: Reflections on the Unborn in American Culture.* Westport, CT: Praeger Publishers, 1996.
Young, Curt. *The Least of These: What Everyone Should Know About Abortion.* Chicago: Moody Press, 1984.

Chapter Five: The Problem with Immigration

Barone, Michael. *Our Country: The Shaping of America from Roosevelt to Reagan.* New York: The Free Press, 1990.
Brimelow, Peter. *Alien Nation: Commonsense About America's Immigration Disaster.* New York: Random House, 1995.
Chavez, Linda. *Out of the Barrio.* New York: Basic Books, 1991.
Harrison, Lawrence. *Who Prospers? How Cultural Values Shape Economic and Political Success.* New York: Basic Books, 1992.
Miller, John J. *The Unmaking of Americans.* New York: The Free Press, 1998.
Novak, Michael. *Unmeltable Ethnics: Politics and Culture in American Life.* 2nd. Edition. New Brunswick, NJ: Transaction Publishers, 1996.
O'Neill, Teresa, Ed. *Immigration: Opposing Viewpoints.* San Diego: Greenhaven Press, 1992.
The Rockford Institute. *Immigration and the American Identity: Selections from Chronicles: A Magazine of American Culture, 1985-1995.* Rockford, IL: The Rockford Institute, 1995.
Schlessinger, Arthur M. *The Disuniting of America* New York: W W Norton, 1992.
Schmidt. Alvin. *The Menace of Multiculturalism: Trojan Horse in America.* Westport, CT: Praeger Publishers, 1997.
Skerry, Peter: *Mexican Americans: The Ambivalent Minority.* New York: The Free Press, 1993.
Sowell, Thomas. *Migrations and Cultures: A World View.* New York: Basic Books, 1996.
Suro, Roberto: *Strangers Among Us: How Latino Immigration is Transforming America.* New York: Alfred A. Knopf, 1998.
Williamson, Chilton Jr. *The Immigration Mystique: America's False Conscience.* New York: Basic Books, 1996.

Chapter Six: The Problem with Education

Atlas, James. *Battle of the Books: The Curriculum Debate in America.* New York: W. W. Norton, 1990.
Bennett, William. *The De-Valuing of America: The Fight for Our Culture and Our Children.* New York: Simon & Schuster, 1994.
Berke, Stephen E. *A Time to Heal: John Perkins, Community Development, and Racial Reconciliation.* Grand Rapids, MI: Baker Books, 1997.
Budziszewski, J. *How to Stay Christian at College.* Colorado Springs, CO: NavPress, 1999.

Coulson, Andrew J. *Market Education: The Unknown History.* New Brunswick, NJ: Transaction Publishers, 1999.

Carter, Stephen L. *The Culture of Disbelief.* New York: The Free Press, 1993.

Cheney, Lynne V. *Telling the Truth: Why Our Culture and Our Country Have Stopped Making Sense—and What We Can Do About It.* New York: Simon & Schuster, 1995.

D'Souza, Dinesh. *Illiberal Education.* New York: The Free Press, 1991.

Gerson, Mark. *In the Classroom.* New York: The Free Press, 1997.

Kors, Alan Charles and Harvey A. Silverglate. *The Shadow University: The Betrayal of Liberty on America's Campuses.* New York: The Free Press, 1998.

Moreland, J. P. *Love Your God with All Your Mind.* Colorado Springs, CO: NavPress, 1997.

Sowell, Thomas. *Inside American Education: The Decline, The Deception, The Dogmas.* New York: The Free Press, 1992.

Suskind, Ron. *A Hope in the Unseen.* New York: Broadway Books, 1998.

Vitz, Paul C. *Censorship: Evidence of Bias in Our Children's Textbooks.* Ann Arbor, MI: Servant Books, 1986.

Williams, Walter E. *Do the Right Thing.* Stanford: Hoover Institution Press, 1995.

Chapter Seven: What Americans Should Do Now

Beckwith, Francis and Greg Koukl. *Relativism.* Grand Rapids, MI: Baker Book House, 1998.

Bennett, William J. *The Death of Outrage.* New York: The Free Press, 1998.

———, Ed. *The Moral Compass.* New York: Simon & Schuster, 1995.

———, Ed. *The Book of Virtues.* New York: Simon & Schuster, 1993.

Boot, Max. *Out of Order.* New York: Basic Books, 1998.

Bork, Robert H. *Slouching Towards Gomorrah.* New York: HarperCollins, 1996.

Henry, William A. III. *In Defense of Elitism.* New York: Doubleday, 1994.

Horowitz, David. *The Politics of Bad Faith: The Radical Assault of on America's Future.* New York: The Free Press, 1998.

Kors, Alan Charles and Harvey L. Silverglade. *The Shadow University.* New York: The Free Press, 1998.

Otis, Don. *Trickle Down Morality.* Grand Rapids, MI: Baker Book House, 1998.

Prager, Dennis. *Think a Second Time.* New York: HarperCollins, 1996.

Sittser, Gerald L. *A Grace Disguised: How the Soul Grows through Loss.* Grand Rapids, MI: Zondervan Publishing House, 1995.

Sowell, Thomas. *The Quest for Cosmic Justice.* New York: The Free Press, 1999.

Sykes, Charles. *A Nation of Victims.* New York: St. Martin's Press, 1992.

Willard, Dallas. *The Divine Conspiracy: Rediscovering Our Hidden Life in God.* New York: HarperSanFrancisco, 1998.

Woodson, Robert L., Jr. *The Triumphs of Joseph: How Today's Community Healers Are Reviving Our Streets and Neighborhoods.* New York: The Free Press, 1998.

INDEX